FOSTERING CULTURE
A Leader's Guide to Purposefully
Shaping Culture

R. Shane Jackson

This book is dedicated to my dad. You taught me much of what is written here and created an environment for me to learn the rest. Thank you for being an incredible father, business partner, and friend.

Acknowledgments

As any author will tell you (and as I have now learned), writing a book is a laborious process. This one has taken weeks of work that has stretched across a few years. It has not and could not have been done alone.

First, thank you to my beautiful wife, Celeste, who allowed me time to write instead of being on the beach.

Patti, thank you for your incredible logistical work in figuring out how to get me out of the office figuratively and literally for days at a time.

Thank you to my proofreaders for your insight and feedback. You made this book much better.

Thank you to Robyn for your excellent work on what is sure to be your first of many books edited.

Most of all, thank you to the amazing leaders in the Jackson Healthcare companies. You are the ones who make what is described in this book a reality.

Shane

Table of Contents

INTRODUCTION

"Can you tell us a little bit about the culture at Jackson Healthcare?"

The question caught me off guard. I had just given a speech for a group of local business leaders, and when I opened it up for questions at the end, I was presented with this query. I found myself talking about the fitness center, the restaurant, the game room, plans for expanding the campus, but I knew this wasn't really answering the question. So, I shifted to the camaraderie among associates, the team service projects, the opportunities for professional growth, and yet still, this felt inadequate. I'm not sure how the person who asked me the question felt about it, but I walked away unsatisfied with my answer. In fact, it nagged me for weeks. The concept of "corporate culture" had really started to trend, and as the face of one of Atlanta's Best Places to Work for 10 years in a row, I knew I was going to get this question again.

It was around this same time that I began taking over more leadership responsibilities from my father. He felt ready to take a step back from the day-to-day operations of the company he began so many years before. The man whose personal values were at the very core of the business was entrusting it to my care. No pressure, right?

Now, I like to think I've learned a thing or two from my dad, having grown up in his house and worked alongside him for 17 years. As he likes to say, "Most lessons are caught not taught," and

I've certainly caught a few. But I didn't want to rely on some innate sense I had about our company's culture and merely hope that would be enough to sustain it. No, if I was to foster the culture and preserve it as the company grew, I would need to be able to define it—not only for myself—but for other leaders throughout the company, who would serve to perpetuate our culture.

So I began a journey of trying to fully understand culture—first in a general sense, and then more specifically, the culture of Jackson Healthcare. Just as one must understand the elemental concepts of addition and subtraction before grasping the advanced concepts of algebra, I knew I needed to start with the basics. I had to understand what culture is before learning how to foster it within our company.

I use the word "foster" very intentionally here. We tend to think of fostering primarily in relationship to at-risk children. Foster parents selflessly take children into their homes to provide care when no one else will. My grandparents were the foster parents of my father. Pulling him out of a horrible situation, they took on the role of encouraging and promoting his development as a young man. Were it not for their interest and involvement in him, he would have been a very different person indeed.

However, the word "foster" has many other applications. The definition of foster is to "encourage or promote the development of something." Teachers seek to foster an environment conducive to learning. Coaches want to foster a tradition of winning.

Perhaps because of my family history, this concept of fostering has stuck with me. As I moved into my current role,

I quickly realized that a primary part of my job is to foster the unique culture that has led to our success. The culture was not wholly created by me, but it would be up to me and the other leaders in the company to promote and sustain it.

Our company has been blessed with tremendous success. As I write this introduction, we are passing $1 billion in revenue. We have outgrown our industry every year we have been in business. In fact, our average growth rate has nearly doubled that of the industry for the past 10 years (an increasingly impressive feat as we have become one of the largest companies in our industry). We continue to operate more efficiently with margins that improve year over year and are far above those of our peers. But in a service business such as ours, revenue growth means headcount growth. And we are literally adding people every day. Amazingly, we have more managers today than there were people in the entire company just a few years ago.

Keeping up with our tremendous growth has presented challenges on multiple fronts—not the least of which is figuring out how to preserve the culture that has, in great part, generated our success.

This brings me back to the journey I set upon of understanding culture so that I might discover how to influence it. This book documents the answers I found and offers guidance to leaders on the ways we can foster our culture.

To understand culture, you have to understand people, and the pursuit of understanding people is psychology—something I necessarily discuss quite a bit in this book. However, you will find very few clinical terms or references to experiments. The statements in this book are merely beliefs I hold based on personal observations, experiences, and a few ideas learned from others. To apply a concept that I will discuss in Chapter 35, they are opinions, not facts.

This book is written in two parts. The first part is a dive into understanding what culture is, and the second is an exploration into what drives the culture of our company specifically. As you'll see, it's my view that one's values and beliefs drive culture. So the second part describes Jackson Healthcare's values and beliefs about how the business should run. Some of these grew out of my own experiences, but many of them were instilled by my father.

If you only have time to read part of this book, read the second part, as you will probably get much more practical use from it. But if you have the time, the second part will be more helpful after the context of the first. It's like learning to play a song on the piano versus learning to play the piano. You can learn to play a song, but if you don't understand the instrument, you won't be able to make music.

My goal is for every leader in our company to have a clear understanding of culture and what drives the culture at Jackson Healthcare, so they may join me in fostering the culture of our great company.

Part I: WHAT IS CULTURE?

1
Artifacts

Jeans. Suits. Open office plan. Closed doors. Telecommute. Child care on site. Free snacks. Fitness center. Do these things explain a company's culture?

When you ask most people to describe the culture of their business (and what I often said before beginning this journey of learning about culture), what you typically hear are examples of manifestations of their culture. If it's a tech startup, they might tell you how they wear t-shirts and play ping pong in the break room, while people working at a law firm describe wearing suits and offices with oak paneling. You sometimes hear about rituals or traditions, such as having kegs on Friday afternoons or potluck meals on holidays.

People may try to explain culture by discussing how the group uses technology. Some groups brag about using technology in the place of physical meetings, while others talk about how they cherish being face-to-face and even forbid the use of email on certain days in order to build relationships.

These answers contain what Edgar H. Schein, author of *Organizational Culture and Leadership*, calls "artifacts" of culture. It's no wonder that we rely on these kinds of descriptions—this is how we have been trained to understand culture from any study of history. Archeology attempts to extract an understanding of ancient cultures by decoding these kinds of artifacts.

Both the ancient Egyptians and the Mayans built pyramids. Based on the artwork and other artifacts found around these pyramids, historians believe that the Egyptians used their pyramids as crypts, while the Mayans used theirs for human sacrifice. Surely that tells us something about the differences between those cultures!

But doesn't this example highlight the challenge we face in understanding culture? We use stories, spaces, traditions, and technology to try to get a sense of what it would feel like to be a part of that group, but these things, these artifacts, don't always reveal why and how the culture came to be.

Another example of the challenge of understanding culture comes from international travel. People often visit other countries to try to experience the culture of that area. I remember talking with a friend who was about to go on a trip to Rome. I asked her what she was going to do while there.

"Oh, I really want to experience the Italian culture, so we aren't just going to see the sights. I want to eat in some local restaurants and really get a feel for the people."

For a moment, let's look past the hubris of thinking one can understand the Italian culture based on a three-day visit. But consider what you do if are going to Rome for three days and want to try to experience what it is like to be a Roman. You visit cathedrals, look at art in museums, eat at sidewalk cafes, shop in small stores, and walk around the city observing people. What you gain from those environments is a view of some of the artifacts of that society. And indeed, those artifacts give you some sense of what it would be like to live there.

But compare those tourists on a three-day trip with a student who goes oversees and lives with an Italian family. Beyond seeing some of the sights that the tourists also see, the student will see how the people in that culture relate to each other. How do they work, play, and treat their family and friends? How and when do they have meals? Do they celebrate birthdays, and if so, how?

Which of these two do you think has a better understanding of the culture? The student, of course, though the reason may not be completely obvious. Certainly, the more time one spends in a culture, the more they will understand about that culture. But gaining a deeper understanding of culture does not derive from merely observing a larger volume of artifacts. The key to really understanding culture is not just knowing about the traditions and ceremonies, the physical spaces that have been created, or how people use technology. To really understand a culture, one must understand why these things exist or have developed the way they have.

To blend into a group's culture, you have to act as they act, which means handling situations the way they would handle them. You must literally and figuratively speak their language. If an occasion calls for a certain kind of behavior and you do something that is contrary to what someone indigenous to that culture would do, you will stick out. If you go to an Italian birthday party and you start singing "Happy Birthday" in English while everyone else is singing a different tune in Italian, no one will think you understand their culture.

A particularly astute student will consciously look for the reasons people in a certain culture do what they do. Looking for the "why" can expedite cultural understanding, but as we will discuss later, if you spend enough time with a group, you will understand why they do what they do—whether or not you can clearly articulate it.

So, it is easy to understand why we have a hard time explaining our own cultures—much less the culture of others. The best we can usually do is describe the things we see that result from a certain culture. But just because you have seen the Coliseum, it doesn't mean you know what it's like to be Italian.

The Culture of Change

A visitor to Rome may also be struck by the visible examples of cultures that thrived and then died. Certainly, the culture of Rome today bears little resemblance to that of Imperial Rome two thousand years ago. What makes some cultures persist and others fail? To be certain, throughout history civilizations have come to power and receded from power for many reasons—perhaps the primary being the invention of superior technology by a rival culture. Indeed, the ancient cultures of Mesoamerica stood little chance when the Europeans showed up with their guns and germs.

But there are plenty of examples of civilizations that had access to the same technology as their rivals, but for some reason clung to the past to their detriment. In what would later become known as the First World War, Germany invaded France with the intention of capturing Paris and forcing the French to surrender. However, France was able to repel them, keeping them out of Paris and ultimately, with the help of their allies, defeating the Germans. Many French credited a new field gun called the French 75 with giving them the ability to repel the German invasion. The gun gained legendary status in France, often being referred to as "Our Glorious 75."

During the period between the World Wars, the French built massive fortifications (called the Maginot Line) on most of its Western border, so they could keep the Germans from invading France again. Their glorious 75s were used all along the line. Thinking themselves now impervious to German attack, the French began drastically reducing their military and all but stopped investing in any further development of new weapons.

Of course, concurrent with the French military downsizing, the Germans under Adolf Hitler began a massive rearmament and development of new strategies that would make the Maginot Line irrelevant. This time when the Germans attacked, it was only a few days before they occupied Paris.

Certainly, the French had access to the same technologies and military thinking that the Germans did. These two groups of people are seemingly quite similar—practically neighbors in Europe, with advanced civilizations, and relatively similar manufacturing capabilities. So, what was it about their cultures that caused the two very different approaches to military technology and strategy?

As business leaders, we are continually thinking about what could happen to our businesses. We want to maintain the things that are working for us but make sure we can change if needed. The French certainly maintained what had worked in the First World War, but they were unable to change. What in our business culture would drive how we will respond to changes in technology or strategy? What should we be guarding about our culture—and what should we allow to change?

2
The First Company

My journey into understanding corporate culture began by trying to understand the "corporate" piece. This may sound basic, but what is a company? If I am going to understand its culture, perhaps I should first understand what "it" is.

After looking at a few definitions of "company" from several sources, here is what I came up with:

A company is an association of individuals who share a common purpose and unite in order to focus their various talents and organize their collectively available skills or resources to achieve specific, declared goals.

So that's a lot of words. Here is a simpler version:

A company is a group of people who have a common motivation to accomplish something that they can't do individually, so they organize themselves and work together.

That makes sense to me. Want to build a train line that crosses the country? Can't do that alone. Let's form a company of people so that we can all work together to do it. Want to sell computers? Wow, I need a lot of different skill sets for that one—engineers, manufacturers, logisticians, salespeople, retailers, just to name a few. I better get a whole bunch of people together who each have one of those various skills, and then get organized so we can actually get a computer designed, produced, sold, and shipped.

Let's break down the elements of this definition:

- An association of individuals with various talents
- Who share a common purpose
- Who organize their collectively available skills
- To achieve specific, declared goals.

In other words:

- Who?
- Why?
- How?
- What?

Let's expand them and arrange them in a different, more logical order:

- What are you trying to accomplish?
- Why are you trying to accomplish it?
- How are you going to accomplish it?
- Who do you need to accomplish it?

Those are really important questions to any organization. But consider this: Couldn't this same framework be applied to civilizations?

Think about human civilization in its earliest and most basic form. Why would families, tribes, or clans join together instead of warring with each other? Groups of people only join each other when they have a common purpose that they could better achieve by working together. When mankind was trying merely to survive, they quickly determined that sometimes they could hunt or gather food more effectively by working together. Let's surround the woolly mammoth and take him down together instead of me attacking him alone. You are good with a spear, and I can throw rocks accurately. Let's get organized so we don't accidentally kill each other. You go left, and I'll go right. Why do we have to do it my way? Because I've hunted these animals before, and I know the best way to do it. Voilà, the first company was born—Woolly Mammoth Hunters, Inc. Let's make Bog bring the mammoth back to camp while we go find another one, and we'll give him some meat for his trouble. Our first employee.

This silly example shows how civilizations began to develop. We need to survive, and many hands make for lighter work. I'll hunt, you cook, that guy will find shelter, and that lady will make clothes. Wait! Who are those people who keep stealing our food? Let's get together with that family across the river—they never steal from us. Maybe we can build an area with a wall around it to store all our stuff. If we work together, we can build a big enough wall that the thieving hooligans can't get in. Hey, we have a village!

The fundamental reason people get together, why civilizations are born or companies are created, is because the people involved have a common purpose. The reason tribes, clans, and nations are created is for the common purpose of survival.

When trying to understand a culture, it is important to distinguish between what is trying to be accomplished and why it is being done. What our little clan is doing is building a wall around their village. Why they are doing it is so that they can protect their food and keep from starving. That's a pretty good purpose statement!

Once you understand how a group has answered these questions of why, what, how, and who, the artifacts of that group make much more sense. As archaeologists uncover the remains of the village we created and discover the base of the wall, they will know that the wall was built for protection. But other artifacts will make more sense as well.

After we build our wall, those marauding scavengers that have been trying to steal our food come up with a new technology. These innovators take two really long limbs, connect them with a series of smaller sticks, lean it against our wall, and then use it to climb up and over. They start using this device to get in and resume stealing our food. It's fairly easy to defend (we just stand on top of the wall and push this crazy contraption over), but these people have the tenacity to come in at night while we are asleep! So, we create a new position—the night watchman. He stays awake all night so that he can alert the village if the marauders try to climb our wall, and we can repel them. The problem is that occasionally the night watchman falls asleep, and the marauders get in. We make a new rule—you have to stay awake while you are the night watchman. We have the first policy manual (which, as all future policy manuals will be, is filled with rules that ought to be self-evident, but amazingly, must be written down). Uh-oh, someone fell asleep and broke our rule. That guy is kicked out of the village. You're fired!

One day a distant cousin comes to visit our beautifully walled village. Cousin Doobie comes from a place where there are no marauders, and hence, no need for walls or night watchmen.

Doobie is impressed by the wall, but he can't fathom its usefulness. Wouldn't the time spent building that wall be better used in some other way, like seeking love and peace in the stars? And he is incredulous that a group of people could be so cruel as to kick someone out of the village merely for sleeping. Come on man, can't we all just get along? He quickly goes back to his home full of judgmental attitudes about the inferior culture of this walled-off society.

Today, we live in a society that has progressed beyond the motivation of mere survival. After centuries of civilization, the vast majority of the population in Western culture has been able to satisfy our basic physical needs to the point that many of our activities are now in pursuit of much more complex psychological and emotional needs (the "whys" behind our "whats"). But just like our mammoth hunting ancestors, we still affiliate with others in an attempt to satisfy some of those needs.

Discerning why a group exists is particularly challenging, and the answer may be slightly different for each person. Most people don't know why they belong to a group—they were born into it or happened upon it. Perhaps it was just the job that was available. To understand why people join groups—or do anything they do—one must look much deeper below the surface.

3
Joining

To more fully understand the culture of a company, let's think about why people join or leave groups in general.

So, let's go back to our village. We've lived here a while now, and the village has grown. In fact, our family and the one from across the river have both had kids, and so we had to extend the walls to create more space for all the people. Sometimes when we leave on hunting expeditions, we see other people and they ask where we live, so they can come trade with us. It sure would be nice to be able to tell them something shorter than "the place with the walls next to the bend in the river." How about Riverwall? Yeah, that has a nice ring to it.

Things are progressing nicely in Riverwall. The marauders keep coming up with new inventions in ongoing attempts to steal our food, and we keep coming up with new methods of thwarting their efforts. After seeing a couple of people kicked out for sleeping on the night watchman job, no one sleeps on duty anymore. Frankly, it's unthinkable that someone would sleep on duty. We've come up with other roles for people that not only help protect our food supply but also increase it. Some of our people built another section of wall surrounding a field where we can plant and grow vegetables. We've created a series of places in the river that corral the fish so that they are easier to catch. We even dug a well so that we can access water in case we are sieged by marauders and can't get to the river. One might say that we have a culture of innovation!

One day, two sets of visitors show up. Being friendly types, we greet them warmly. Turns out each group is a family looking for a place to live. We have a lot of work to be done in our growing village, so we invite them to settle.

The first family is from a village a few miles away that was also regularly attacked by the marauders. Instead of building a wall, their village created a series of traps where they could ambush and defend against the marauders. Like us, each person in their village took turns watching out for attacks at all times of night. Unfortunately, one night the marauders were able to go around the traps and overcome the village defenders to steal all of their food. After this attack, the family decided to come to Riverwall.

The Trap family (as we started calling them) fit in quickly. Even though they came from a village without a wall, they took naturally to serving turns as night watchmen, and they pitched right in with the hard work of hunting, fishing, and farming. Eventually they learned how to do maintenance on our ever-growing wall. In fact, the Traps became so respected that people listened to them when they showed us how to improve our walls by adding traps to them.

The second family did not come from a village but had lived with a group of wandering nomads. This group didn't farm, but instead would live off what the land naturally produced. After they had depleted the resources of one location, they would move on to a different place that could support them. We took to calling them the Grazers. The Grazers had also been attacked by the marauders, and since they had no defenses, they were easily defeated, often losing all their food. Like the Traps, the Grazers came to Riverwall because they were seeking safety from the marauders.

One advantage of being nomadic is that it gives you a lot of time to be with your family as you emigrate from place to place. As a result, the Grazers put a lot of importance on their family, and particularly, the time they could spend with their children. Since their lifestyle required them to reside in places that were producing food and game, they were always in warm locations. This meant that they were used to adjusting their work schedule around the heat of the day. Now these seemed like fine traits, especially the bit about placing importance on their family. The problem was that the Grazers did everything differently from us.

Not only were they not good at farming, they had difficulty even grasping the concept of why one would want to farm when there were lots of plants around that provided plenty of things to eat. Since they had never been in a village, and therefore never been through a siege, they couldn't understand why you would need to drink water from under the ground. But their inexperience in these areas was just part of the problem.

While the residents of Riverwall would work all day utilizing the good light to see, the Grazers would seek shelter during the heat of the day, saying that midday was for teaching their children. Besides, they argued, this left them better rested to work during the early morning and evening when it was cool and one was more effective.

A few days after the Grazers arrived, the elders of Riverwall sat down with them to explain the rules of living in the village.

Each person was expected to farm and hunt to provide for their own family, but they were also expected to do work that supported the village as a whole, such as perform maintenance on the wall. The Grazers were flabbergasted by this concept. Never before had they worked for anyone other than their own family. Still, they wanted protection from the marauders, so they tried to fit in. They began to take their turns as night watchmen. But they did so begrudgingly and eventually began complaining about how being so tired from the night watch negatively impacted family time.

Frustrated and feeling like his children were not getting the attention he wanted to provide, the head of the Grazer family set off on a journey to see if he could find a better place to live. A few weeks later he returned and told his family that he had found another walled village full of people who only worked in the morning and evening. They immediately packed their things and moved to that new village.

As soon as the Grazers left, the rest of the village breathed a collective sigh of relief. The Grazers never seemed to do their work to the same level of quality as everyone else. They just didn't fit in, and it would be much easier without them there.

The Traps and Grazers illustrate that there is something deeper at work behind why people do what they do. Both are trying to accomplish the same thing of providing their families with food, shelter, and safety. Yet one puts the needs of the community ahead of the needs of their own family, while the other does the opposite. Both accomplish their work but use different methods of getting the work done. Said better, they place value on different things and have differing beliefs about how things should be done.

What we are discovering here is that becoming part of a culture requires more than sharing a common purpose. It is more than agreeing on what needs to be accomplished or even how it needs to be accomplished. One coming from outside of a culture has to become acquainted with and integrated into the why, what, and how in order to become a part of the who.

One coming from outside of a culture has to become acquainted with and integrated into the **why, what,** and **how** in order **to become a part of the who.**

If every group must answer these questions in order to form as a group, what determines how people answer them? Why would the Traps and Grazers, who shared a purpose in protecting their families, have such differences in how they went about it? Because the way one answers the questions of why, what, and how is determined by his or her values and beliefs.

"They Just Don't Fit In"

This is the phrase I hear most often about people who fail at our company. The vast majority of people who join our company understand our purpose and what we are trying to accomplish. We rarely lose someone who says, "Wow, I didn't know you were in healthcare!" or "I didn't know you were trying to save people's lives through your work!" Certainly, there are people who don't have the skills to do the job at a sufficient level. But most of the time, it's because they have different beliefs as to how the work should be done. Even if they adopt our methods, you can tell that they do so begrudgingly. They stand out and cause angst on their teams. They don't treat their coworkers or customers the way everyone else does or communicate like their teammates do. And when they leave (or are asked to leave), everyone is inevitably relieved.

4
Values

Your values and beliefs determine your decisions, actions, and how you see the world. They determine the information that your brain accepts and ignores. Differences in values and beliefs are the reason that two people can view the exact same event and have different impressions of what happened. Values and beliefs are largely unconscious, and yet they exercise tremendous power over us.

Something this powerful is worth understanding. Let's start with values.

Values are one of those things that we feel like we understand but are hard to describe. Ask someone about their values and you are likely to hear things like honesty, integrity, or faith. Others may talk about valuing family, conservation, or fitness. But what does it mean to value one of these things?

At its base, value is the worth that we assign to something. It is anything that we hold in high regard because of its importance to us. We value things because they are useful to us in satisfying some need. We value having money because it enables us to purchase the things that meet our needs.

To help us understand values, let's go back to our visitors, the Traps and the Grazers. Before coming to Riverwall, the Traps lived in a situation where their physical needs were met by virtue of being a part of a community. While they certainly loved their family, their experience led the Traps to place great value on the community. The Grazers, on the other hand, were part of a community of nomads that was loosely affiliated and constantly changing as people came in and out of the group. This led the Grazers to place tremendous value on the immediate family as the only people they could depend on.

Even when both families were living in the relative safety of Riverwall, with its secure walls and plentiful supplies of food and water, the psychological values of community and family still drove much of their behavior. These competing values of family and community determined how they viewed their situation—the Traps viewed work done on behalf of the community as essential, spending as many daylight hours as possible in work. The Grazers saw midday work as taking away from the time necessary to teach their children, and thus, counter to the value they placed on their immediate family.

One point that is apparent here is that the priority of values is important. It wasn't that the Traps didn't value family—they did. It wasn't that the Grazers didn't see the value of work—they did. But the Traps place greater value on working in the community, and the Grazers put greater value on family, and that difference in priority caused a huge difference in behavior.

What about values such as integrity or honesty? Do you think that the residents of Riverwall value integrity, when their very lives depend on the night watchmen being true to their word and staying awake through the night, even though no one is watching?

Our friends in Riverwall are focused on physical safety and sustenance. Indeed, these are the primary drivers for all people.

When your physical safety is threatened, everything else in your consciousness is pushed to the side until the threat is over. When you don't know where your next meal is coming from, nothing is as important to you as figuring out how to eat.

Unfortunately, many if not most of the people in the world today live in circumstances that are not all that different from the ones in Riverwall. For them, the daily quest for their personal survival and that of their lineage drives their behavior.

However, once physical needs are met and a degree of certainty around physical survival is achieved, people quickly move on to other values that are geared to achieve emotional and psychological survival. These are principles or standards of behavior in which we place great worth, not because they give us physical safety, but psychological safety.

The need or desire for physical survival is hard-coded, and every person has that need by virtue of being alive. Psychological needs are more often a product of our circumstances, most particularly the circumstances of our childhood.

The children who grow up in the Grazer family will more than likely have a lifelong value of family that will shape their actions— just as the Trap children will value community. Most likely neither will be aware of these values, or if they are aware of them, they may not know why they have them.

Our little parable of Riverwall begins to fail us when we consider what creates the values of the majority of people in developed nations today. Many people in these cultures have never experienced a time when they had to make decisions primarily for the purpose of physical survival. Their values were shaped primarily in pursuit of satisfying psychological needs. So, while the Traps valued the community because it meant physical well-being, someone today may develop a value of community because it helps them feel like they belong or gives them an identity.

I'm not going to delve too deeply into how values come into being for each person; I'll leave that for the real psychologists. However, I think it is helpful to understand that everyone is seeking a sense of worth in themselves. We value things that provide that sense of worth. This may be a personal trait such as integrity or humor, our friendships or romantic relationships, our wealth or beauty, or any other number of manifestations.

It is also helpful to understand that these values are pretty hard-coded and incredibly difficult to change. Many studies have shown that the core values that are associated with your self-image and drive your behavior are largely set by the time you are seven years old.

Finally, I think it is also important to state that most people do not know what they value, much less why. Either they haven't explored it deeply enough, or they aren't being honest with themselves. If you subscribe to the theory that your values and beliefs determine your decisions and actions, then it follows that your decisions and actions will reveal what you truly value.

If someone claims to value honesty, but lies regularly, would you question if they actually value honesty? In fact, they probably do place some value on truthfulness, but there is something else that they value more that becomes a priority to them over honesty. For instance, if a person is in a situation where they can improve their popularity by lying, it simply means that they value popularity more than honesty.

If an honest person is in a situation where they are faced with the decision of lying and saving a child or telling a truth that will lead to the child's death, which value will receive higher priority? Honesty or life? If they choose to lie, does that mean they don't value honesty?

Let's use a less ugly example and one that isn't a hypothetical—in fact, it is highly relevant to most business people. Not too long ago I was involved in a discussion with a group of business leaders about time management. We began by talking about methods to become more effective in how we organized and prioritized our activities. However, it soon became a discussion about how often all of us find ourselves doing something that ostensibly has little value to us. We've all been there—we have something really important to do, but instead of doing the important thing, we do other, unimportant things. The student who has a term paper due, but instead of working on it, spends an hour playing video games. The salesperson who has a big presentation to give, but checks email instead of preparing for it.

Why do we spend time on these activities that seemingly offer no value? I would argue that, in fact, they do have value. Even if something is urgent, you will not do something that has no value to you.

Let's take a ridiculous example to prove this point. Right now, as I type this, there is a daytime soap opera that is about to be telecast on TV. If I want to watch it, I have to act at this very moment. I haven't set a DVR to record it, and it won't be available on demand later. It is now or never—the definition of urgent. And I couldn't care less. I am not going to take any action on it because that soap opera has absolutely no value to me.

However, while I was typing that last paragraph my nine-year-old daughter came into the room asking me about a charger for an electronic device. I paused from my typing to respond to her. Now, in the grand scheme of things, I believe that this book is going to be more important and valuable than my little dialog with my daughter about a charger. However, because I value our relationship, I chose to engage with her instead of ignoring her. Now that wasn't a conscious decision; my mind just knew what to do in order to satisfy my psychological need of having a good relationship with my daughter.

Whatever action we take is because our minds are trying to solve a physical or psychological need. You aren't checking your email instead of preparing for a presentation for no reason. Your mind is trying to solve some need (like perhaps creating the feeling of accomplishment by cleaning out your inbox).

So, does this mean that we just go on instinct, and whatever we do or feel in the moment is what we should be doing? Of course not. As we mature, we understand more and more that some things yield far more value in the long-term than others. Maturation is a process of broadening and lengthening our view of value—of recognizing the difference between momentary pleasure and the joy that comes from physical and psychological satisfaction over long periods.

As children, we readily give way to our impulses. There is sugar available? Eat it. There is a game to play? Do it. As we mature, we start to understand that while that sugar tastes good in the moment, it is secondary to the sedentary feeling that comes later. When we start to see the health problems associated with our expanding waistlines, we place more value on the long-term benefits of health and less value on the instant sugar rush.

The key is to bring more and more of these decisions to a conscious level. Just as we consciously decide to place less value on the sugar rush, we can also decide that the feeling of accomplishment we get from checking email is fleeting compared to the long-term benefits of nailing a presentation for a client.

So the next time you find yourself doing something that seems out of sync with what you believe your values to be, reflect on the need that action is meeting and be honest with yourself about the value you place on that need, compared with those values you espouse. If you believe your espoused value really is superior, change your behavior.

Sounds simple, right? The painful truth is that most people place maximum value on the pleasure of the moment. Subsequently, their life is simply a continual and repetitive pursuit of pleasure which is, by its nature, fleeting and short-lived. They don't know it (or more accurately, they won't admit it), but the pursuit of pleasure drives most behavior for most people.

So why take this detour into psychology in a book about corporate culture? Remember that any group—and for our purposes, a company—consists of a group of people who have come together to achieve a specific task in a specific way for a common purpose. The values of the individuals in that group will determine whether they share the purpose that defines the group (the what), whether the task is something they want to solve (the why), and whether they agree to the way the task is being done (the how). Their values determine whether they opt into or out of the group, or whether the group invites them in or asks them to leave.

As a business leader, it is important to know that those who join your business are doing so to fill a personal need. It is their purpose for being there. However, it is the level of alignment between their personal values and those of the company that determines whether or not they will stay.

Generational Difference in Values

My grandparents were part of what Tom Brokaw labeled the "Greatest Generation," those Americans who lived through the Great Depression and then defeated the Axis powers. Their formative years took place in a time when a huge portion of Americans lived with uncertainty around where tomorrow's meals would come from. Then they lived through a war where everyday goods were rationed so that one had little certainty as to the availability of goods, even if you could afford them.

Is it any wonder that my grandparents, along with many of their contemporaries, were incredibly frugal and seemingly never threw anything away?

I remember being at their house as a child and wandering through the room that served as the pantry, storage closet, and laundry room. There were countless random objects in that room. Most of that stuff, if it were in my house today, would be discarded immediately. When my grandmother passed, it took weeks to go through all of the items stored in the attic.

Compare that to people entering the workforce today. Indeed, some of them come from meager financial backgrounds, but that portion of the population is nowhere near what it was in the mid-20th century. The current generation has largely spent their lives pursuing the fulfillment of psychological needs, not physical ones. Their communities as adolescents included anyone who had access to social media, compared to previous generations where geography determined community. Is there any wonder that their work, communication, and relationship habits might be different?

Does this mean that people from different generations cannot be members of the same group? Of course not. But leaders must focus on those values that overlap.

5
Beliefs

Merriam-Webster defines a belief as "a state of mind in which trust or confidence is placed in someone or something." I'd add that beliefs are formed because of a conviction that someone or something is true, good, right, or valuable. By implication, one can also hold beliefs that someone or something is false, bad, wrong, or worthless. Beliefs guide our actions, often to the same degree as our values do.

To understand beliefs, it helps me to think about what I call the continuum of defense. On one side of this continuum are the ideas you would literally die to defend. On the other side of the continuum are ideals you agree with, but they are not as important to you. I will defend the belief, but not at great cost. In the book *Change the Culture, Change the Game*, authors Roger Connors and Tom Smith helpfully classify beliefs into Categories 1, 2, and 3, with Category 1 beliefs being highly malleable, and Category 3 beliefs being incredibly hard to change.

As an example, when the Traps moved to Riverwall, the citizens believed that simply having a wall was sufficient for defense from marauders. However, once they learned about the additional protection yielded by traps, they altered their belief about what provided the best defense. Conversely, the Grazers would not give up on their belief that it is better to work in the morning and evening, because it was a belief that hit closer to the value of family.

It is worthwhile to identify your beliefs personally and professionally, but when doing so, it is especially valuable if you can place them on the continuum of defense. Which are those beliefs that you feel so strongly about that it would take incredible force to dissuade you or to get you to act against them? Which, if any, of your beliefs are really preferences? All things being even, you will act consistently with those beliefs, but if the breeze is blowing the other direction, then you won't have much discomfort in abandoning them.

To some, the notion of a belief that is so easily abandoned sounds like heresy. These people view life as binary—something is right or wrong, good or bad, true or false. If it is true then it is always true and worthy of defense.

Let's go to an absurd example to prove this point. Like all sophisticated, intelligent people, I believe that banana pudding is best served cold. A problem occurs when I am at a family event and my mother has prepared homemade banana pudding, but made the awful mistake of serving it right out of the oven. I begin to present the evidence that has led to my belief in the virtues of cold banana pudding, yet amazingly, it does not dissuade her. There is now a dent in my belief that all sophisticated, intelligent people see the superiority of cold pudding, as my mother is herself a sophisticated, intelligent person. I am now faced with the dilemma of pressing on with my argument, refusing to eat the pudding at sub-optimal temperature so that I am living consistently with my beliefs, or discarding my beliefs and eating the warm pudding so that I don't hurt my mother's feelings. Since I place more importance on my relationship with my mother than the temperature of food in my mouth, I dig into warm pudding.

Certainly, in this example I am really referring to a preference and not a serious belief, but the point is that we hold more tightly to some beliefs than others. Our loosely held beliefs are often more a question of taste that we will easily abandon, compared to the deeply held beliefs we hold true.

Here is a business example that is perhaps more illustrative. I believe that first impressions are important. Once we create an impression, it is hard to change that perception. Because we as a company put so much focus on the personal level of service we provide to our customers, I like the people who visit our company to experience a similar level of service as soon as they walk in the door. As a result, we have a person whose job it is to greet everyone who comes to our office and help take care of their needs. Now, some of our smaller offices around the country don't have anyone there to greet people when they walk in. Perhaps they have a bell to ring so someone can come out to help. Do I think they are wrong and insist that they put someone by the door? No. I could give them the argument as to why it is valuable, but it is not a belief I hold firm on in every situation.

It is important to know your beliefs because, like values, they will drive how you act, make decisions, and see the world. And also like values, they will determine who is ultimately a part of your group or company.

Let me demonstrate how this plays out by giving a very personal example. For some deep-seated reasons that I won't take time to explain, I put a lot of value in "having a good name," or being respected by others. Consequently, I place a lot of negative value on others thinking poorly of me. I define having a good name as people thinking of me as someone who lives in a way that is consistent with my espoused values. For example, I value integrity—doing what I say I will do even to a point of great expense. It is therefore important to me in our business that we deliver on our promises to our customers. I have various beliefs as to how this is accomplished, but at the most basic level, I believe that we should always do whatever we tell our customer we are going to do. If we tell them we will call them on Friday, we do it. If we tell them we will give them a certain price, even if we later learn that selling at that price means we will lose money on the deal, we will honor the price.

Now, let's take a hypothetical business leader with a different set of values. This person has a great psychological need for security. Perhaps because of living in an environment of uncertainty as a child, he is driven to create an atmosphere where he feels safe. When he was young, he witnessed people who had wealth and seemed more secure than he was. As a result, he formed the belief that wealth would bring him security. He values money as a way to meet that need.

He also believes that every person is out to protect their own and that each interaction is an isolated event where someone wins and someone loses. So he sees every business transaction as an opportunity to secure as much wealth (security) as possible. He places some value in integrity, but not at the cost of losing wealth. He also believes that there are plenty of people in the world, and so he doesn't care if the people he has done business with in the past don't trust him and won't work with him again. He only needs to do business with enough people to secure his wealth, and then he won't really care about what other people think of him.

I'm not making a statement about which of these sets of beliefs is right, wrong, good, or better. The point right now is that they are very different, and the two cannot coexist in a group. I can tell you that the hypothetical person I described would not survive (and would not want to survive) in my company, nor me in his.

Let's continue with this example as a way of illustrating the different levels of beliefs on the continuum of defense. As I said earlier, I believe that if you tell someone you will call them on Friday, you should call them on Friday. Don't email—call. However, someone else in our company may make an argument that, in a certain circumstance, an email is a more effective communication tool than a call because it will better communicate the information that the client needs. I would probably yield on this argument and let the person send an email, because my belief about literally doing what you say you will do is not as strong as my belief in the principle of integrity.

Actually, I would probably suggest they call to tell the customer that they have sent an email.

Your mind is constantly seeking out and testing things that may satisfy your physical and psychological needs. When things work or don't work, it records that information. The more often or more severely that same thing works or doesn't work, the more the mind believes in that causal relationship. It encodes these relationships—both positive and negative—as beliefs.

Think about how this could impact the way someone communicates. One of the most basic human psychological needs is to be understood. Let's say a child is seeking to communicate something to his parents, but can't get their attention. However, when he yells and screams, they will finally listen to him. The next time he wants to be heard, he remembers that the yelling and screaming worked and so he does it again, and voilà, his parents hear him. Guess what his default mode is going to be in the future? He believes that the best way to be heard is to yell and scream at his parents. It makes you wonder how the belief in the positive value of yelling and screaming will impact communication patterns later in life!

Let's take a business example. If a business manager has tried pay-per-click advertising in the past with no success, it will be difficult for the marketing team to convince him to do it another time, even if the circumstances have changed. It didn't work in the past, and his mind has already formed a belief that PPC doesn't work.

It is also worth understanding that your beliefs shape not only how you see the world, but what you see in the world.

One of the jobs of your mind is to seek a state of stability. Your brain is constantly reconciling your beliefs about the world with the reality of the world. To admit that the world is not as you think it is causes great trauma for your mind. The stronger you hold the belief, the harder the mind will work to defend it. For a very strongly held belief, the mind will change your perception of the world before it will change the belief.

Unfortunately, people in abusive relationships exhibit this phenomenon. A woman who believes her husband loves her will ignore the verbal and even physical abuses for a long time before admitting that her belief is wrong. It is incredibly hard for children who have been abandoned to reconcile that reality with the belief that they are loved by their parents. Beliefs are powerful things.

This desire of the mind to reinforce its beliefs drives personal and professional behavior. If I believe my coworker is incompetent, everything I see him do demonstrates incompetence. If I believe that the product I am selling is the highest quality, I will seek information that confirms that and ignore or discount information about the quality of my competitors.

Think about the last time you listened to someone giving a speech that you really liked. If you walked away from the speech thinking that the speaker had done a good job, there is a good chance that your primary recollections were about all the good points she made that were in alignment with what you think. If she said things that weren't consistent with your beliefs, you probably quickly forgot about them. If you are a note taker, chances are you wrote down only the things you agreed with. If you are one of those people who writes down everything a speaker says, you may be surprised to go back and see in your notes things you don't agree with.

Author and speaker Lou Tice describes this phenomenon as a mental scotoma. In medical terms, a scotoma is a blind spot in an otherwise normal field of vision. Someone with a scotoma can see normally in most places, but they have one place where there is nothing there. Mental scotomas work similarly; I see normally except in the areas where I have strongly held beliefs. In these areas, I have a blind spot to the evidence that contradicts my belief.

Mental scotomas can be fixed, but doing so causes great discomfort. Being faced with overwhelming evidence that convinces me my beliefs are wrong means that my brain has failed in doing its job of reconciling my picture of the world with the reality of the world. Being aware that the brain works this way helps, but it is still a challenge to overcome. When you are blind in an area, you don't see the danger that lurks in your blind spot.

The brain doesn't just avoid information that contradicts your beliefs, it actively seeks out information that confirms them. The brain is constantly seeking evidence that confirms its view of reality. That's why you remember the parts of the speech you agree with. That's why when you read a paper you go to the articles that "interest" you.

This act of seeking out confirmation isn't just limited to facts in speeches or articles. It plays out in the choices you make about the people in your life. Think about your friends or your significant other. More than likely, the people you are closest to hold values and beliefs that are highly aligned with yours. When we say that we have a lot in common with someone, we are really saying that we have similar values and beliefs.

This impacts organizations that we affiliate with. Would you choose to become highly involved in a church if its teachings were at odds with your beliefs about the nature of God? On the contrary, I know many people (including myself) who have spent lots of time "church shopping," visiting numerous churches trying to identify the one that most aligned with their beliefs.

Do we even need to talk about dating?

Our beliefs shape how we think things should be or ought to be done. Our brains constantly seek to reinforce our beliefs by seeking out confirming information and ignoring information that contradicts. Unconsciously, we seek this confirmation in our relationships with the people around us. This determines our friends, who we date and marry, the organizations we affiliate with, and yes, the companies we choose to work for.

Negative Value

"I hate losing more than I love winning."

I have seen many athletes credited with this quote — tennis great Jimmy Connors among the first. However, I will tell you that it could have been me who said it.

As a child, I was fiercely competitive. (I am still competitive, but maturity has done away with some of the negative behaviors associated with competitiveness.) I would do almost anything to win, but mostly because I didn't want to lose. Even a tie was okay, as long as I didn't lose. In fact, I hated losing so much that if I didn't think I could win at something, I wouldn't participate. If I was playing a board game and it became apparent I wasn't going to win, I would quit without finishing (often knocking the game and its pieces into the air to announce my decision to quit).

We give items both positive and negative value. You can think of it this way—you would pay money for something you desire, but you might also pay money to avoid something undesirable. Theme parks have picked up on this in charging people for special tickets that allow you to skip the lines for certain rides. These customers place such negative value on waiting in a line that they will spend money to avoid it. Perhaps one could argue that they are placing positive value on their time and spending money to maximize that value. However, if you ask them why they bought the special ticket, I guarantee you will most often get the answer, "to avoid standing in line."

Indeed, negative values often correspond to something we positively value, but the negative value might outweigh the positive in importance. I value having fun with my family, but not enough to take the beating of spending all day standing in hot lines with other stinky, sweaty people waiting for a ride that lasts 45 seconds.

Don't underestimate the power of negative values in shaping our beliefs and behaviors.

6
Group Dynamics

Let's think about a local church:

- Everyone is there voluntarily (well, at least the adults).

- The members choose to be there because they agree on some basic core beliefs.

- Each individual is wired to seek out information that confirms their beliefs.

- Each person is now surrounded by others who are also wired to confirm those same beliefs.

It's not surprising that a group composed like this is really good at reinforcing their beliefs. In fact, the beliefs of a church are so ingrained that they use a different word for them: doctrine. And people who disagree with them have a truly disagreeable label: heretics.

I'm not picking on churches here. (I belong to one!) The point is that when you have a group of people who have high alignment on values and beliefs, they will get really good at entrenching those beliefs. Edgar H. Schein refers to these as "assumptions"—beliefs that are so ingrained that they are taken for granted. You find very little variation inside a group about assumptions—people rarely stray from them. They are high on the continuum of defense. You may have also heard the term "common knowledge." It's common knowledge because everyone just knows that it is true—there is no need to even discuss it.

Don't interpret this as a bad thing. Assumptions are necessary for survival. If you couldn't assume anything, you would be overwhelmed with the number of decisions you would face. I assume that if the light fixture worked yesterday, it will work again today. If I couldn't make that assumption, it would take me a lot of time to test the lighting mechanisms each day.

Assumptions lead to group norms that enable a group to work more quickly. If I know that the accounting department needs to see data in a certain way in order to process it, it soon becomes normal for me to provide the data for them in that format every time. To do otherwise would be wasteful of time and effort.

Group norms of communication are especially useful. If I know that our group has a stand-up meeting every morning, I have confidence that I will be able to convey or receive information at that time. Otherwise, I would have to go to people individually to figure out how to effectively communicate every time. If I know that our group normally communicates via email and, subsequently, people check email often, I have confidence that I can communicate with the group when I send an email. In our company, it is understood that if your email is really long no one will read it—an important thing to know if you have something to communicate!

More important norms of communication involve style and not just mode. In an organization where there is a shared belief in directly communicating bad news, the members will talk very directly with each other. Someone who beats around the bush will cause frustration to the others. In a group that places high value on honoring each other and believes that pointing out mistakes diminishes honor, members will address bad news indirectly and only in private—if at all.

As I have stated before, the point here is not to cast judgment on which of these is better. The point is that they are different. Someone taking the communication style from the first group and using it with the second group will be ineffective at best and highly offensive at worst. However, people within the group who share the values and beliefs that are driving the communication style of the group are able to communicate within the group effectively.

As we said earlier, the mind places value on things that meet a physical or psychological need. It develops beliefs about the things that repeatedly work to solve those needs. The same thing can be said of groups.

Individuals bring beliefs to a group, but the group will also develop beliefs about things that solve problems for the group. The more often and longer that those things work to solve a group need, the more ingrained they become as beliefs, the closer they get to becoming assumptions, and the more the group will defend them.

One time we had a competitor that our salespeople believed operated so poorly that they were regularly angering and running off clients. The competitor's operational problems were such common knowledge on the sales team that the pitch they used whenever competing against this company was based on this belief.

One day, after hearing for the umpteenth time that the other company operated poorly, I asked the sales manager, "Would you agree that if XYZ Corp is operating that poorly, they would be losing market share?"

"Well, yes," he said, "I'm certain they would be."

"So, if they aren't losing market share, is it possible that their service isn't as bad as you think it is?"

"Well, we all know they have terrible service."

Now, prior to this conversation I did something novel. Knowing the competitor was a public company, I went to the internet and pulled up their financial statements. I then presented him with irrefutable proof that the other company was in fact growing and not shrinking.

Not wanting facts to get in the way of his belief, his response was that the competitor was obviously slashing prices in order to make up for their bad service. I then pointed out that they had nearly identical margins to ours. Well, that could only be because the clients have been tricked and don't know any better! And so, the defense of his closely held belief about the competitor continued.

There is both power and danger in strongly held beliefs. A group that is highly aligned on its values and beliefs can work very efficiently and effectively. This is especially true when a group has been together for a long time with repeated experiences that reinforce its beliefs. You hear about these groups that can "speak shorthand" and "know what each other is thinking." They get things done quickly because they have so many common assumptions that there is less to communicate. When they communicate, it is in the style that is most consistent with their beliefs, which is readily accepted and understood by everyone, and therefore very effective.

This has a great impact on how you think about integrating a new person into a team like this. If their personal values and beliefs do not align with the group's beliefs, it will be very difficult for them to succeed within the group. Someone will have to change or act against their beliefs. And people will only tolerate acting against their beliefs for so long. If you have a group of people who have strongly held beliefs that have developed and been reinforced by repeatedly seeing those beliefs satisfy their needs, and you introduce a new individual with opposing beliefs to that group—who do you think is more likely to change? Who is likely to leave?

Just like the mind seeks stability, so do groups. The mind is looking for ways to reinforce its beliefs and reject things that contradict its beliefs; groups do the same thing. Imagine a successful team that has been together for a long time. That group has developed a practice of opening their calendars to each other so that they are all aware of what each other is doing. A new person comes onto the team who has had an experience on a team in the past where everyone's calendar was opened and it led to resentment, as people saw that others weren't working the same number of hours. He believes that this practice will eventually lead to the demise of the team and tries to convince the others of this. If this is a strongly held belief, the group will seek all the reasons why their team is different and he is wrong. It will be really hard for him to convince them otherwise. He will either change, leave, or get kicked out of the group.

This often plays out at strategic levels of organizations. Our company believes strongly in the power of specialization. (I'll say more about this in the latter part of the book.) This belief is high on the continuum of defense, so executives who have come to work for us who believe in being generalists have not lasted very long.

Groups are their own unique organisms. They learn, think, reject, and accept. While they are a product of the people in them, they develop values and beliefs of their own as they seek to solve both the individuals' needs and the group's needs. Like people, the group will protect its beliefs, and an individual's participation in the group will be predicated on his or her alignment with the group's beliefs.

7
Good vs. Bad

Let's start by giving a definition to corporate culture. You may be sitting there thinking, "Finally, he's actually going to say what corporate culture is. I sure wish he would have put this chapter first—then I wouldn't have had to read all those previous chapters!"

My intention with those chapters was to provide a basis for recognizing what culture is such that we understand it without really needing a definition. But just to be sure, let's define it as it relates to companies, if only to make sure we've covered some of the nuances.

So, remember my definition of a company?

A company is a group of people who have a common motivation to accomplish something that they can't do individually, so they organize themselves and work together.

And remember the four questions this definition implies all companies must answer?

- What are you trying to accomplish?
- Why are you trying to accomplish it?
- How are you going to accomplish it?
- Who do you need to accomplish it?

We concluded that the values and beliefs of a group determine how it will answer those questions—and that the members of the group will join or leave the group based on their individual alignment with the group's values and beliefs.

Of course you remember all that. So, you will probably not be at all surprised at my definition of corporate culture:

Corporate culture is the atmosphere that results from the actions a company takes to accomplish its purpose based on its people's collective values and beliefs.

I like this definition for a couple of reasons. 1) Substitute the word "corporate" for "family," "national," or any word describing a group, and the definition still works. 2) The word "atmosphere" is useful. In this context, we aren't talking about the gases that surround the planet. Atmosphere is the pervading tone or mood of a place or situation. It's something you just feel. When you hear a sports announcer say that the atmosphere in a stadium is "electric" you know that they are trying to describe the feeling or mood of the place. Cultures yield those kinds of metaphysical descriptions.

In 1992, I had the opportunity to spend a month in Russia. This was a huge deal for me. I was a teenager and managed to get excused time out of school. Some of the time I was in Moscow, but mostly I was in a city called Barnaul in Siberia. This was shortly after the communist government of the USSR had fallen, and the group I was with was one of the very first groups of Americans to travel to Barnaul.

To say that the atmosphere in Russia in 1992 was different from what I was accustomed to in the United States would be a gross understatement. The Russians are a people who have lived under tyranny for centuries. From the czars to the communist dictators, the ongoing oppression fostered suspicion, betrayal, suffering, and hopelessness. I remember being amazed at how different the eyes of the Russian people were from Americans. There was no light in their eyes—especially the older people. The mood was dark and guarded. When you rode the subway system in Moscow it was deathly quiet—no one uttered a word or looked at the other people on the train[1]. The energy was completely different.

One of the things we often hear from people who visit our offices is how they can feel the energy as soon as they walk in. They comment about how friendly and helpful people are—even talking to each other on the elevators. Often when I interview candidates who are applying to work at our

---

[1] The only exception to this was a few of the young people I met who had hope for a new democracy. Those people inspired me and reinforced my belief in the superiority of a democratic system of government.

company, I get questions about why this is so. As I mentioned at the beginning, these questions are what led to this book. Visitors sense something different in the atmosphere at Jackson Healthcare, but what?

Using our new definition of corporate culture, we understand that the atmosphere of a company is the result of all the decisions the group makes about running the business—how they treat customers, how they communicate with each other, how the workspace is designed, how they recognize achievement, how they define achievement to begin with, and on and on. And the way the group comes to those decisions is driven by its values and beliefs.

If you look at most of the literature written about corporate culture, the vast majority of it differentiates "good" culture from "bad" culture. But applying labels like "good" and "bad" to a culture requires us to make a judgment about that organization based on one's personal values and beliefs.

For example, consider those companies with a reputation for having a "competitive culture." These companies are known to hire the best of the best and then pit them against each other in a battle over who can deliver the most innovative ideas and the highest quality work. This approach has led to the growth of many companies that are considered highly successful, but I personally wouldn't want to be a part of a competitive culture. I value teamwork and collaboration too much. Does this mean a competitive culture is bad? No, but it is very different from what I would consider ideal.

If you had asked me in 1992 if the culture of Russia was good or bad, I definitely would have said it was bad—and no doubt, the Russian culture was a result of centuries of rule by often truly evil people. However, thinking about it now, I can see that my negative response to the culture was largely due to the ways it was different from my own. At that time, for me, different equaled bad—which of course is not always the case.

The **more relevant question** isn't whether a group's culture is good or bad, but **how effective it is in accomplishing its purpose**.

That's not to say a culture cannot be bad. I believe that many cultures (both geographic and corporate) have developed at the hands of evil people who valued despicable things. The societies and cultures that grow out of evil beliefs reflect that evil. Certainly, any culture in which individual lives are disposable is, indeed, bad. And on the corporate front, any culture in which people willingly harm others in pursuit of personal profits (Enron comes to mind) is also bad.

However, those are extreme examples. So, putting aside those who actively seek to do others harm, the more relevant question isn't whether a group's culture is good or bad, but how effective it is in accomplishing its purpose.

8
Strong vs. Weak

If you accept that the true measure of a culture is its effectiveness in accomplishing the group's purpose, then it is worth understanding what makes one culture more effective than another. In this chapter, I will argue that a strong culture is more effective than a weak one at accomplishing its purpose.

Cultural strength is a measure of the intensity of cultural identity and alignment. Strong cultures have highly adopted, consistently shared values and beliefs among its members. In contrast, weak cultures have little adoption of shared beliefs where disparate individual values often trump group values.

Strength of culture is a function of:

- The percentage of the group in agreement about
- The priority of and
- The number of values and beliefs.

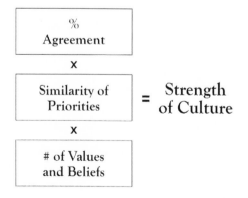

Or think of it this way: As we explored in Chapter 4, the priority of values matters—as does where beliefs fall on the continuum of defense. For a group to exist, there must be some agreement on its most highly prioritized values and eagerly defended beliefs.

It may be helpful to start with weak cultures to help us understand the formula.

What would happen in Riverwall if each family had disagreed on the best way to defend against the marauders? Some believed a wall was the best defense, some others thought they should live in trees, and still others thought they should live on an island in the river. How likely do you think it is that the villagers would have stayed together? Not very.

However, even when there is agreement on the highest priority value and beliefs, if there isn't agreement on the lower held values and beliefs, there could still eventually be a split in the group. Remember the Grazers? They believed in the basic value of protecting their family from the marauders and even came to agree with the belief that the wall was a good way to accomplish that. However, their other beliefs did not align with the rest of the village. They placed a much higher value on spending time with family than everyone else. As soon as they heard about another village that could provide for their safety and also allow them more time with their family, they left the village.

Bring this back to a business setting. Aside from the independently wealthy, people work to survive. We could say that they have a shared value of eating and sleeping indoors. Every company exists at its base level to provide for the survival of its owners and employees. So if you are the only employer in town, you can get away with relying on only this shared value to keep people working for the company. It doesn't matter how badly you treat people, they will keep working for you because they don't have another choice. However, as soon as there is another employer who provides alignment on even one other value, you will lose your workforce.

Groups with strong cultures have lots of people who similarly prioritize many values and beliefs. To further illustrate this, let's think about geographic cultures.

When I was in Siberia in 1992, it was evident that this was a group of people searching for answers. They were part of a country whose government had failed to meet even the most fundamental needs of its citizens. After decades of struggle, they had finally thrown off the shackles of the communist regime and were seeking something new.

Compare this with the United States. Sure, we argue over lots of disparate values and beliefs (just look outside the White House at the new protesters who camp out every day), but we haven't had an attempt at a government overthrow in 150 years. For the most part, the United States provides for its citizens' most basic needs and values (at least compared to the rest of the world). It so happens that a lot of people identify with the values of freedom, liberty, and justice. People go to extraordinary lengths trying to get into the US—to join its culture, not to escape it.

So why is the strength of culture so important? So far in this book, I have tried only to educate, not persuade. However, at this point I'd like to make the argument that a strong culture is worthy of pursuit. I am not trying to convince you of any specific values and beliefs that would lead to a particular culture, merely that groups with a strong culture are powerful.

I would argue that strong cultures are able to achieve the goals of the group better than weak cultures because strong cultures lead to increased loyalty among members and increased consistency in the way things are done.[2]

The stronger a culture, the more loyalty the members of the group will display towards the group. In fact, the loyalty of group members is perhaps the best measure of cultural strength. Strong cultures successfully achieve their purpose, so its members are loyal because their needs are met. Weak cultures are signified by a revolving door of group membership and little adherence to cultural norms by the members who are there.

---

[2] A geopolitical example of this is happening in Europe today. Like America, Europe is experiencing mass immigration from other countries. But unlike the US, these immigrants are not assimilating into the culture of their host country but maintaining pockets of their previous country's culture. Compare this to the US, a country entirely comprised of immigrants, where the second generation of immigrants typically identifies more with US culture than the culture of their parents, and the third generation often has no affiliation with their previous culture whatsoever. The lack of alignment in Europe is causing tremendous social issues there compared to the US.

The **loyalty** of group members is the **best measure of cultural strength**.

The Russians overturned their government because it could not provide its people's most basic needs—physical or psychological. Governments of prosperous nations are much less likely to be overturned. Many of the European monarchies fell during the 19th and 20th centuries because they were unable to provide for their citizens due to the wars they fought against each other that caused famine and widespread destruction.

Wait, famine? War and destruction? So, your company may not elicit global socioeconomic consequences, but if you have really high turnover in your business, it might feel like war and destruction! I've never met a business leader who believes high turnover is good for their business. Most everyone understands the loss of productivity and quality that comes from having to train someone new to do a job because the last person left.

Quality is defined as the standard of something as measured against other things of a similar kind. In other words, quality is based on consistency. How consistent is this product with the other products? How consistently do members of a group handle similar situations?

When there is great alignment and adoption of values and beliefs, there is a higher propensity for things to be done in a similar fashion. As an example, people in our company have a high alignment around the value of serving others and the belief that providing a good outcome for the customer leads to long-term business success. As a result, customers are highly likely to receive the same quality of customer service, no matter who they interact with in our business.

Compare this to another organization where, depending on who you deal with, sometimes you get good service and sometimes you don't. That inconsistency is likely to annoy customers and ultimately drive them away.

My guess is that you have worked in a place like this—where people are really just there for a paycheck. They adhere to the company policies so that they keep their job, but when a rule isn't strictly enforced, they do their own thing. No one goes above and beyond. Comments you hear in places like this include "everyone has their own agenda" or "it's highly political." Ask someone in one of these companies and they are likely to tell you that they are always looking for another job. People spend little time together outside of work, and when they do, it's often to complain about their jobs.

At companies with strong cultures, people talk more about what the group is accomplishing than what they accomplish as individuals. They brag to their friends about where they work and refer their friends for jobs. Working from similar belief systems, they quickly make friends with coworkers and spend quality time with them both inside and outside of work. They fiercely defend and help each other out of a desire to see their friends succeed.

They do excellent work because what they do is a reflection of who they are and what they believe.

People are loyal to groups, or even companies, when they share the same values and beliefs. To the extent that a loyal group is desirable in achieving its collective goals, a strong culture should be pursued. How can a leader create a strong culture? I'm glad you asked.

The Berlin Wall

For decades, people living under communism sought to escape their countries and flee to the West. The communist governments went to extreme lengths to keep their citizens from leaving—executing those trying to escape so as to dissuade others from attempting to leave. The most famous example of this is probably the Berlin Wall.

When Germany surrendered in 1945 to finally end the European part of World War II, the armies of the four Allied countries (the United States, the United Kingdom, France, and the USSR) had all reached Berlin and were residing in different areas. With no local government intact, the victorious armies ruled over the section in which their armies were residing. These four zones were soon consolidated into two—those of the Western countries and the Soviet zone.

During the reconstruction of Berlin that followed
the war, it soon became evident that the philosophies
of the democracies compared to the communists
were completely different, and their effectiveness in
returning the area to prosperity was drastic. At first,
people could still live in their homes in East Berlin and
go to the West to work. But eventually, many people
sought to move across the city to the Western zone
where they would have better opportunities to work
and provide for their families.

The East Germans looked at their problems—and
how much they were falling behind the West—and
blamed the issues in the East on the greedy people who
were fleeing. How could they improve their area if the
people kept leaving? Why couldn't they think about the
good of the community and not just themselves? To solve
this—and stop these selfish people from leaving—East
German officials stopped allowing people from the East
to go to West Berlin. Their people were so determined
to flee the desolation of East Berlin that they would go to
extreme lengths to get there, causing the East Germans
to eventually build a wall manned with soldiers who had
orders to shoot anyone attempting to cross.

I have often wondered about those governing East
Germany. It seems that the Mayor of East Berlin would
have realized that everyone living in his city was trying to

go somewhere else because their needs couldn't be met where they were. Wouldn't you think that at some point, instead of blaming the people who were trying to leave, he would see that the other side was better at providing for its people, and that perhaps his side ought to change the way they govern?

However, I think it is fair to turn that question to ourselves. How often do we vilify those who leave our companies? When people leave, are we blaming them instead of the system that can't meet their needs? Are we relying on contracts and legal threats to keep our people working for us? What walls have we built to make our people stay?

9
Role of a Leader

It is often said that the culture of an organization is a reflection of the leader. Especially in small or startup companies, the culture is based on the values of the entrepreneur.

Based on everything we have discussed in the book so far, this makes sense. The founder of a company starts the business for a specific purpose that is consistent with his or her values. He applies his beliefs about what strategies and tactics will work to the operations of the business. She hires people who believe in her "vision"—what she wants to accomplish and how she is going to do it. He is doing the work alongside the other people in the business, who are trained by watching how the founder does things. She makes managerial decisions consistent with her values and beliefs, and everyone in the business does things her way. Very quickly the people adapt to the written or unwritten rules of the founder, and all the decisions surrounding the business are made based on those rules. Eventually people just know how the founder wants things to work, and they don't have to ask or be told anymore. The atmosphere directly reflects the group's adherence to these norms. Unconsciously, all decisions in running the business are based on the founder's values and beliefs.

But then the company grows. Now the founder doesn't manage everyone directly. And while the other leaders agree with the founder on the big things (or else she wouldn't have hired them), they have different opinions on some of the lower priority values and beliefs. Things start to change a little. While mostly consistent, people who work for the new managers do things just a little differently than the original group. Eventually, the company grows to the size where there are lots of new leaders, and most of the people who work for the business have never even met the founder. Every team has a different style or way of doing things based on what that group's leader believes is the best way to get things done.

I often hear comments from people who have worked for a company that has gone through this cycle about how they miss the "old days." They reminisce about how when the company started everyone worked so well together; they were like a big family. Since the company has grown, they say things just aren't the same.

These are very valid comments that are worth analyzing. Using our model of culture, it would make sense that a small group of people organized by a founder for a specific purpose, who all agree on a set of values and beliefs, would be a really tight knit group with a strong culture. As others come in with different values, that culture starts getting diffused. As the culture weakens, the new people aren't as committed, and the people who felt such a strong connection with the original group start to lose some of their loyalty. And with so many different ways of doing things, quality and consistency of service start to decline.

Anyone who has ever worked for a successful startup has experienced this—it is one of many reasons that it is so hard to scale a business.

Later in this chapter, I'll discuss how you can apply this model as a leader at any level of an organization. So if you aren't a founder or CEO, hang in there with me. But I want to start by talking about how senior leaders should think about this, because the lessons are applicable to both.

I am assuming that if you are still reading at this point, you agree that having a strong culture leads to superior business results based on higher consistency, quality, and loyalty of the people involved in the business (which includes both employees and customers—but this too will be discussed later).

So how do you overcome the natural inclination for culture to weaken as the business grows?

One of my favorite lessons that I learned from my father (and you will read a lot more of them in the second part of this book) is that I can't disagree with your decision until I understand the information and assumptions you had in making the decision. For example, if your friend told you that they decided to pull their child out of school yesterday, you may think that your friend is being an irresponsible parent, doesn't value education, and is setting a bad example for their child. However, if you learned that there was a bomb threat at the school, you'd probably understand how they came to their decision. The value they placed on their child and their belief that the child was in danger led to their decision and action.

For a leader, understanding the culture model is the key to understanding and influencing people's behavior. People's decisions are based on their values and beliefs, so the only way to change their decisions is to change their values and beliefs. This, of course, is not easy. But when you view your job as a leader through that lens, it provides a tremendous amount of clarity about how to be effective as a leader.

As discussed earlier, our core values and beliefs (especially the beliefs we have about ourselves) are set at a very early age. It is incredibly difficult, nay impossible, to change someone's core values or highly defended beliefs. A much easier way to build a group of people who agree on values and beliefs is to start with individuals who already agree on values and beliefs. This sounds ridiculously obvious, but in fact, it requires leaders to change the way they think about hiring. The focus should be to find people who identify with the company's values and beliefs who are also technically competent. This is the first application of the culture model.

The problem is that most interview processes are designed solely to determine whether someone can do the technical aspects of a job. While technical competence is certainly important and necessary, it's not sufficient. An interview process must be designed to reveal a person's core values and beliefs. Compared to this, interviewing for technical competency is a walk in the park. In Chapter 27, I will talk about our approach to interviewing, so I won't go into an exhaustive discussion here. The point to understand now is that interviewing must be designed to determine a person's cultural fit—their identification with the values and beliefs of your group.

The second application of the culture model involves how you spend your time with people in your business.

My job as the leader of the company is to make sure our people understand our vision (what), mission (why), strategy (how), and how our values and beliefs impact the way those are executed. Every interaction I have with people in the company is intentional in executing that job.

So when I am in a one-on-one meeting with a leader discussing strategy, my goal is to help create clarity around how our beliefs impact that situation. When I interact with someone who is on the front line of our business, I try to discuss how our values impact the way we deal with customers. When I send out companywide communications about a given situation, I emphasize how our values were upheld in that situation. When I speak to new hires, I discuss our mission and how it impacts what they will experience as a part of the company.

As I said earlier, if someone has differences on core values, they most likely won't change. But most people become malleable on lower priority values and beliefs and can be influenced—especially by someone they respect. Further, for the people in your business who do align with your values, there is a lot of openness to discussing how those values are applied throughout the business.

The third application involves how you define and measure success.

As the old adage goes, what gets rewarded gets done. If the only way you measure success is based on the bottom line, guess what you really value? You can't say you believe in making the customer happy and never measure or reward customer satisfaction.

This applies at both the company level and the individual level. We measure our leaders against our values and a multi-faceted definition of success. To be promoted in our organization you have to be successful at all of them. Again, if you give the highest profile to the person in your company who drives the most sales, but treats others with disrespect, everyone else knows what they really have to do to succeed.

One time we had an office that beat their profit budget for four straight years. However, compared to other teams in the company, they had the lowest customer satisfaction scores, the highest turnover, and the lowest scores for treating others in accordance with our values. All of these were clearly communicated as indicators of success—just like hitting budget. So, I shut them down. Not surprisingly, we saw an immediate jump on all the other teams for each of these indicators. When it comes to our values, we mean what we say.

So all of that works fine if you are the head honcho, but what if you are a team leader who reports to someone who reports to someone else who reports to a guy who reports to the head honcho? What impact can you have? A big one.

Years ago, the person in our company who ran our new hire orientation asked me to stop by to say a few words (this was before I began doing this regularly). He just asked me to come into the meeting whenever I had a chance that morning.

When I walked in, he said, "Oh what great timing! I was just explaining our culture!" Sure enough, I looked up at the slide on the projection screen, and it was full of platitudes about our values and the environment of the company. Then he asked me, "How would you define our corporate culture?"

I answered, "My definition of corporate culture is how your boss treats you. It doesn't matter what we say here, because if your boss treats you like crap, then for you, the culture sucks."

He never invited me back.

Now, that was many years ago, and as you now know, my definition and understanding of corporate culture has developed quite a bit since then. However, there is still a lot of truth in that statement.

Just like the founder of a company sets the culture for that initial team, you as a leader determine the culture for your team. The way you communicate, the direction you give, what you reward (even if just with your praise), everything you do is creating the atmosphere on your team. And just like a founder, there is much value for you in understanding the culture model and creating clarity on values and beliefs within your team in order to impact behavior. If you work in a company with a strong culture and clearly articulated values and beliefs, then you have these resources at your disposal. If not, then what a great opportunity to make your own mark!

There is never going to be total alignment between two leaders on values and beliefs—and that is not only okay, but also helpful. Within our business, we have an overarching culture with many subcultures among the various teams. The ideal situation is where there is alignment among leaders on core values and beliefs, and then each leader will apply them in slightly nuanced ways. This is where innovation and best practices come from.

Whether they realize it or not, every leader is directly impacting, if not setting, the culture of their team. The only question is whether you are doing so intentionally or accidentally.

10
Applications

The more you understand the source of culture and begin to recognize what drives the behavior of individuals and groups, the more applications you will see. The applications for leaders discussed in the last chapter are just the beginning. Your understanding of culture impacts nearly everything about how you lead and how you relate to other people. This chapter provides more applications and lessons learned from the culture model. They can be applied in business, of course—but also in everyday life.

Be Honest About Your Values

I mentioned this earlier, but many of us have been in places that had values on a poster that hung on a wall, and we knew they were just that—a poster on a wall. The words had nothing to do with how decisions were made.

If you agree with the premise that your decisions are driven by your values and beliefs, logic implies that if someone regularly watches you make decisions, then they will be able to determine your values. So, regardless of whether you ever speak about them, the people who work in your business will know what your values are.

Several years ago, a college professor came to do a study on our company. His research was on the correlation between strong corporate cultures and market outperformance. It's important to note that this was before we ever wrote down, much less talked about, what our values were. He interviewed almost 20% of the people in the company and asked them to describe the culture and values. Amazingly, the answers were highly consistent. Even though we didn't talk about them, people knew what our values and beliefs were.

The worst thing you can do is claim to believe one thing and then act in a contradictory manner. That is called hypocrisy. People have always despised hypocrites, and in our highly evolved society, perhaps more so today than ever. Hypocrisy is a surefire way to sow the seeds of disloyalty in your business. So ask yourself, "If you were on trial for your values, would there be enough evidence to convict you?"

Decide Where You Will Compromise

This is not meant to be a misleading header. When you hear about someone compromising on their beliefs, you may get a negative connotation. I think of someone succumbing to negative influences and going to the dark side. While that is certainly to be avoided, that's not what I am referencing.

This really comes down to spending time thinking about the priority of your values and beliefs. For example, I definitely value honesty. However, like the example I gave earlier, if I am put in a situation where my child will die unless I tell a lie, then you will see me lie through my teeth. I value the life of my child more than my own honesty.

As an aside, when I use that little example about lying to save your child, it makes a lot of sense to some people and typically offends others. Some people will say that they are honest no matter the consequences—and bravo to them for putting so much priority on honesty. The difference in reaction really just proves the point that people prioritize values differently. (And I hope the offended people are never asked by their spouses if their pants make them look fat. They will surely not like those consequences!)

Let's consider something a little easier to digest. I think it is incredibly worthwhile to list out and prioritize your business beliefs and then consider the ones you would compromise, given the right situation. For example, we believe that it should always take at least two people to approve money being sent out of the business. It is just a good practice to keep people out of potentially questionable situations. It would have to be a really extreme situation to get us to compromise on that belief.

That is an easy example with which few people would disagree. But all smart business leaders have beliefs about how business should be done that other smart business people would disagree with.

Here's a better example. I know many good managers who are big believers in quarterly management objectives. They demand that everyone on their team have clearly articulated goals for each quarter and that some of their compensation should rest on whether or not those goals are achieved. I know other good managers who don't like quarterly objectives— the time period is too long or too short, doesn't leave enough flexibility for change, or doesn't provide the opportunity to focus on longer-term objectives.

The question is if you are a leader who believes in quarterly objectives, would you allow a leader who works for you to manage his team without using quarterly objectives? Is that a belief you are willing to compromise or not?

See how this works?

One thing that has helped me is the idea that principles are sacrosanct, methods are not. Like most leaders, I have my methods that I believe work. However, there are other leaders in our organization that have different methods. My rule is that as long as the method is consistent with the principle (or value or belief), then I am not as concerned about whether it is my method or not.

Principles are sacrosanct, methods are not.

Share Your Values With Customers

Think about what the app stores have done to consumer expectations. I download an app (for free or a marginal cost) and expect it to do exactly what I want. If it doesn't, I delete it and go download one of the other 100 apps that does the same thing. This experience has infected the way we view every product or service. There shouldn't need to be a price negotiation because I can go online and find the best price in the market. If you won't give it to me, I will go buy it from someone else with little additional effort. Today, customers expect the best price and perfect quality every time.

At the same time, technology has separated us like never before. Virtual offices replace physical ones. Texting replaces conversations. Video chat replaces face-to-face visits. We can contact anyone at any time, yet we are hardly connecting with anyone. With their basic physical needs met, people are seeking to satisfy deeper emotional needs of belonging. They are desperate to connect with other people whose values are congruent with theirs. That is the new paradigm of customer service.

For perhaps the first time in history, customers on a mass scale are seeking out vendors who share their values and making purchasing decisions based on these shared values. Shared values are now a differentiator.

Consider how you can authentically share your values with your customers. If you are true to them, you will attract extremely loyal customers. Be careful though, because the only people who hate hypocrisy more than your employees are your customers.

Question Your Beliefs

Wait, what? Haven't we just spent thousands of words talking about the need to clarify your values and beliefs so that we can create strong cultures of people who align with them? Now you want me to question that?

Absolutely.

Our beliefs are based on old information and assumptions. Until time stops this will be true. A curious, driven person will seek to have the best information possible in making decisions. This means that you should constantly challenge whether the assumptions that drive your beliefs are still valid.

Remember our discussion of scotomas in Chapter 5? We all have them, but we can develop the discipline to seek them out and challenge them. One of my favorite exercises is to write down all the rules that govern the way we do business, and then ask what would happen if we broke those rules. Some of our greatest innovations have come out of this type of exercise.

That said, this is in no way meant to infer that you should change your beliefs willy-nilly. Just don't be afraid to challenge even your most closely held beliefs.

One of my favorite quotes is by 19th-century pastor Charles Spurgeon. He said, "The Word of God is like a lion. You don't have to defend a lion. All you have to do is let the lion loose, and the lion will defend itself."

The point is that if something is true, it will hold up to scrutiny. And the more that something is tested and passes the test, the more reason you have to believe in it. If it doesn't hold up then it is either not true now, or it never was. Either way you are able to operate on a superior belief moving forward.

11
Lingering Questions

The next section of this book will lay out the values and beliefs of Jackson Healthcare. But before moving on, I'd like to address a couple of lingering questions that I'm guessing at least a few of you have.

Some intelligent person who has been taught his whole life the value of diversity has spent the last several chapters grappling with some version of this question: if everyone in a group believes the same things, doesn't that lead to a bunch of inbred group-think with no new ideas, and ultimately, to being conquered by another group with superior technology? Well, yes. Next question?

Just kidding.

It is an insightful question and one worth thinking about so that it can be prevented.

I would argue that it depends on the values and beliefs around which the group coalesces. By nature, all organizations are designed to reinforce their values and beliefs. For businesses, this translates as building more and more resources to deliver on a set business model. This is called efficiency, scale, and quality. These are all concepts that are designed to improve an existing model, thereby reinforcing it.

However, if a group shares the value of innovation or believes in the power of challenging the status quo, then a group will be constructed to evolve. In my opinion, these are values that very few people actually have (because of the cognitive dissonance they cause). Therefore, recognizing that an organization's natural design will be to reinforce their existing business model and ignore anything that discredits their beliefs, leaders must be especially vigilant in establishing disciplines that will challenge those beliefs. I give examples of some of those in the second part of this book.

The other question I will address is how to determine what you actually value.

I have found that very few people know what they value. Most people just don't think deeply enough or take the time to consider the question. They act upon their values, they just don't do so consciously.

Of the people who claim to know their values, a small percentage of those people are actually honest about it. The hypocrisy may not be intentional—it may be self-deceit—but their actions belie values that are different from their claims.

As a leader, if you don't know what you value and believe, then I don't know how you would intentionally create a culture around those values. Again, people will discern what your values are because of your actions, but they will then know something about you that you don't know about yourself.

I have utilized several different methods in trying to identify my values, and I think it's important to help people that work at our company do the same for themselves. We ask everyone who comes to work for us to go through a process in new hire orientation of sorting through a list of values to determine their three most treasured. It's pretty challenging to figure out what to eliminate when you have to choose between things like integrity, honesty, wisdom, and charity.

A few years ago, my dad discovered a method that I think is pretty powerful and worth considering.

Remember the professor I mentioned who was doing research on our company? After he interviewed all the people in the company, he met with my dad. In the meeting, he asked him to talk about his childhood. This set him back somewhat. My father had a particularly difficult childhood that had him in and out of the foster care system, and frankly, he doesn't like to talk about it. However, the professor pressed, and so he went into the story. Then, the professor asked another question.

"What values would you have wanted in your family?"

As my dad says, that question hit him like a ton of bricks. That's when he realized that the values he had tried to instill in the company were the ones he had wished he had in his childhood family. Suddenly it became easier to articulate the values that drive our culture. Shortly thereafter, we started posting them on walls.

So, if you are trying to figure out what you really value, what you would want your company or team to emulate, the values that you would want those around you to share, you might consider asking yourself this question: What are the values I want in my family?

Then all you have to do is live them.

Part II: WHAT IS OUR CULTURE?
The Values & Beliefs
of Jackson Healthcare

Values

Several years ago, my father went through an exercise of articulating the values that drive how he makes business (and personal) decisions. Since then, these statements have become visible parts of Jackson Healthcare. We evaluate associates at all levels around these values, and they have become the standard for how we strive to behave in any situation.

Over time, the words we use to express the values have evolved, but the concepts have never changed. They are the same ones that my father taught me as a young boy and that he articulated for the business years ago. But we have adapted the way we state them to make them more memorable and useful in decision making.

In short, the three values that drive us are: Others First, Wisdom, and Growth. But we like to explain them this way: Others Before Self, Do the Wise Thing, and Keep Getting Better.

We are not implying that these values are superior to others or that if you espouse different values, you are inferior. You can choose to adopt these values or not. However, if you are thinking of working in our company, it is important that you know what these values are so that you will understand how we make decisions about the business. To be a leader in our company you must have some basic level of agreement with these values. So, let's dive in.

12
Others Before Self

This one is first on the list for a reason. If we could only choose one value to represent what we believe, it would be this one—think about the needs of others before your own. It is the highest priority value we have. When there is a conflict between values in a given situation, Others First will win. The very reason for the existence of our company is summarized and derived from this value—to improve the lives of other people. I believe that this value drives the primary reason that people come to work here—a desire to not only make money, but to make a difference by serving others.

If you were to summarize this value in a word, it's "love." Not the kind of love you use to describe the goofy feeling we get when we think of someone attractive. We are discussing the virtue of love, defined by Merriam-Webster as the "unselfish, loyal, and benevolent concern for the good of another."

But this is not just some touchy-feely concept. Others First serves double duty for us as both a value and a belief about how to do business. It drives not only our behavior toward others, but also our business philosophy. For example, thinking about your customers' needs before your own tends to lead to incredibly loyal customers. Want to attract and retain really high-quality people on your team? Think about how to serve their needs, wants, and desires.

Note that this doesn't say Others Only. This is not some romantic idealism implying that everything we do is for the good of others and the detriment of ourselves. The idea is that you consider the needs of others before your own, but not to the exclusion of your own. The famous sales trainer Zig Ziglar said, "You will get all you want in life if you help enough other people get what they want." If you can really understand what is in the best interest of someone else, you then have a path to provide them something truly valuable. Ironically, Others First is the ultimate strategy to achieve your totally selfish goals.

However, I would submit to you that living a life focused on serving others is a reward unto itself. A life spent only pursuing your own desires at the expense of others is a lonely, unfulfilling existence. You can only eat so much food, drive in so many cars, or sleep in so many houses. These things are fleeting. Serving others yields lasting consequences that create fulfillment in this life and beyond. There is nothing more rewarding than truly helping someone else.

So let's look at the different elements of Others First and consider how this value plays out in our culture.

Respect For The Individual

An Others First mentality starts with a recognition of the value of an individual person. A person is valuable because they are. Each person has been uniquely created with specific traits, skills, and gifts. Personal value is not determined by a number in a bank account, a position on an organization chart, or membership in a group.

This view of the value of a person is unique and relatively new when you consider the history of mankind. For virtually the entire history of humanity prior to the Enlightenment (which led to the founding of the United States), it was accepted that some people were more valuable than others because of their strength, wealth, education, race, religion, or nationality. It is hard for us today to comprehend how truly revolutionary was Thomas Jefferson's declaration of a self-evident truth "that all men are created equal, that they are endowed by their Creator with certain unalienable Rights." Thankfully, the definition of "all men" has grown over the centuries to truly include everyone— well, at least everyone who is a United States citizen.

It is hard to comprehend that a huge portion of the world's population still lives in an environment where societies and governments condone or enforce racism, slavery, and caste systems. Wars are being fought all over the globe between races or tribes where the victor will commit unspeakable atrocities to the losers and will be held to no account. Western cultures may have made progress in the recognition of the sanctity of the individual life, but we are unfortunately still unique in the world.

It is easy for us to look back on previous generations or other societies with condescending superiority, as we have moved beyond societally condoned slavery and institutionally entrenched classes. However, we often still exhibit the attitudes that led to these horrid institutions. Our behaviors belie our lack of belief in the value of each individual person. How often do we show great honor and deference to people who have occupations that our society has deemed with high regard, while ignoring those who work in lower paying jobs? How many managers have you seen who act one way around the boss and another way around their employees? Unlike other cultures, our society has no formally established class systems, but we often treat people as if we do.

I dare you to ask yourself this question: "What behaviors would I change if I truly valued every person I encountered?" Or even more powerful: "How would I act if I believed that other people have the same value as I do?"

In our company, respect is lost, not won. I respect you because you are intrinsically valuable and able to uniquely contribute in a way that no other person could. The quickest way to lose my respect is to show that you consider yourself more valuable than others.

The importance of this value has deep roots for my family. My father's childhood was spent in the squalor of poverty as he lived with an alcoholic single mother. He was eventually pulled out of this situation and into the foster care system, living in an orphanage, and then ultimately, with a family of foster parents.

If there was anyone in mid-20th century America who could be seen as second-class, as less worthy than others, it was this poor kid from the streets of Atlanta. I sometimes wonder what would have happened if someone had not seen him as worthy of their time and energy. If they had not shown him that he was valuable in and of himself, he certainly would not have turned out the way he did.

If there is any value that I inherited from my parents it was this one—that every person is valuable and worthy of our respect. For if a poor kid from the streets is valuable, then so is everyone else.

Treat Others As You Want To Be Treated

It's not called the Golden Rule for nothing. Jesus says that this one sums up all of the laws of the Bible, so regardless of your religious beliefs, it's probably worth considering.

As kids, we were told that if we want people to be nice to us, we should be nice to them. If we don't want others to steal things from us, we shouldn't steal from them. That was the explanation many of us received of the Golden Rule, and while those things are true, as adults, the applications are (or should be) a bit more complex.

For example, when you face a difficult conversation with someone, ask yourself how you would really want to be treated in that situation. *Really*.

How often do you find yourself wondering what someone's real agenda is? When you are dealing with other people in a tough situation, wouldn't you love to understand everyone's true motivations? Well, if that's what you would want, how often do you declare your honest intentions to others? Imagine being in a negotiation and someone saying, "Let me just tell you exactly what I want out of this deal so that we can figure out if we can both be successful." Wouldn't that lead to a better outcome?

If you were getting fired, what would you want the person firing you to say? Would you want them to just give you the platitudes designed to minimize conflict as you leave, or would you really want to know what happened and why you were being let go—which would ultimately help you in the long run? And yet, what did you tell the last person you fired? Or even worse, what did you tell that person in their last performance review? Were you forthcoming with them? What would you have wanted someone to say to you while you were being evaluated?

The power of the Golden Rule is that it shines a light on the inconsistency of our behavior. We complain about a lack of transparency by others while hiding the truth ourselves. We want recognition for our accomplishments while downplaying the accomplishments of others.

I cannot count the number of times I have screwed up. On countless occasions I have offended someone either accidentally or out of neglect. If you have ever done that, what did you want the offended party to do? If you are like me, you were hoping for forgiveness and an openness to creating a solution for the future. However, when we are offended, how often do we hold grudges against others? Perhaps next time we are offended, before we respond, we remember that many times we are the offending party.

Those with only a surface level understanding of the Golden Rule may have problems applying it in the workplace. For example, many people who are blunt in their feedback get a reputation for being rude. If you ask them, they will tell you that they really appreciate it when people are blunt with them, because they don't have to waste time reading between the lines. That's great, but not everyone communicates that way. When you really consider how you want to be treated, it means that you want people to communicate with you using your preferred style. Therefore, to follow the Golden Rule, you should use their preferred style to communicate with them—which may not be the style you'd prefer. Not exactly what your grade school teacher taught you, huh?

I distinctly remember an argument I once had where after an hour of talking at each other, we finally figured out that the whole argument was because the other person had a false assumption about something I had done or said. I remember thinking how if he had just understood what had really happened, we would have never argued. There is a lot of power in author Stephen Covey's adage, "Seek first to understand before being understood." This is an expression of the Golden Rule and an Others First mentality. I was reminded of this the next time we argued, and it was me who was jumping to conclusions without really seeking to understand.

I want anyone who is important to me to understand me. I dare say we all feel that way. So, if it is important to me to be understood, I need to seek to understand others.

The Golden Rule is a great filter to use when considering every interaction with others—if that were me over there, how would I hope that the other person would act toward me? If you can crack that, you will communicate and build relationships like never before.

Esteem The Team

"There is no limit to what a man can do or where he can go if he does not mind who gets the credit." This quote was on a plaque that Ronald Reagan kept on his desk while he was President. There are several theories but no definite proof of who originally coined this phrase. So, appropriately, no one person gets the credit for this quote.

Business is not an individual sport. In our complex world, a team is required to accomplish anything of importance. If you are going to be successful in business today, you must be able to work with others.

I remember being on a sports team as a teenager with one kid who was an amazing athlete. Clearly, he was the best athlete on the team, and in case you weren't clear on that, he would tell you. If we won, it was because of him. If we lost, it was because everyone else on the team was terrible. His attitude single-handedly sank that team. We had the talent to win a lot of games, but the team was so fractured by this one ego that many of the players didn't play hard, and we lost to teams with half the talent.

Great players make those around them better. And great coaches certainly do the same. Notice what the best coaches do—the ones who lead teams that not only win games, but also generate great loyalty and respect from their players. Listen to what they say after games. If they lose, it is the coach's fault. If they win, their players really played well.

Great teams know that there are going to be ups and downs during the season. They know that there will be some games when a player really plays well and some games when she is just off. But as teammates, they support and encourage each other through it. And they play harder for each other because of it.

What if you were the one who missed the shot, forgot the assignment, or dropped the ball? The crowd boos and you feel terrible. But your teammates rally around you saying, "We're still with you. Forget about it—we know you'll get 'em next time." How much loyalty would you feel to that team? How hard would you work for them?

The reality is that it doesn't matter how good the star player is; in team sports everyone must do their job or the team cannot win. Even Michael Jordan didn't win a championship until he figured out how to be a teammate that raises the level of those around him. In business, and certainly in a service business like ours, every person must do the job the right way for the customer to have the experience we desire. No person on the team is more important than any other.

I occasionally get a question from people who are coming into our organization about what they need to do to be successful in our company. This is the answer I give every time: don't worry about seeking credit for your successes. If you are productive in our company, I guarantee that you will be noticed. You will succeed here if you can make your team successful.

We value teams not just because each person on the team has inherent worth, but because teams can accomplish what no one person can do alone. So, whether you are the coach, the star player, or the role player, if you want to be successful, you need the whole team to be successful. Figure out how to support and encourage your teammates, and you drastically increase the chances of that happening.

13
Do the Wise Thing

Look at any list of corporate values and you are bound to see words like honesty, integrity, or fairness. (And if you don't, you should probably be a little nervous.) Certainly, we seek to honor these values and for years used the phrase "Do the Right Thing" to summarize our desire to act accordingly.

However, that phrase always felt insufficient. Of course we believe everyone should do the right thing, but the question, "What is the right thing to do here?" wasn't often particularly helpful.

The challenge is that in reality we are rarely faced with decisions that are clear choices between right and wrong. Should I steal? Should I lie? Of course these are things that we struggle with, but in general, those aren't the kinds of problems we face, and frankly, aren't the hardest ones.

The harder decisions (and the ones that are far more frequent) are the ones that are not between good and bad or right and wrong, but between good and better or bad and worse. They are not black and white, but varying shades of gray.

It's hard to remember the last time I faced a decision with a clear moral choice—if I take this path, it is right; if I take that path, it is wrong. In comparison, I seem to face questions daily where there is no right answer. Let me give you an example.

I love to hike and camp. I live near the mountains of North Georgia, and within a short drive from my house, I can be on the mountain trails for a multiple-day camping trip. When I hike, I often have choices regarding which route to take to get to the next camp.

Ever since my kids have been strong enough to carry a backpack, I have taken them on hiking trips with me. When my oldest son was 10, I took him up to North Georgia on a hike that would take us to part of the Appalachian Trail. We set out on the drive, but through a series of frustrating events, we got delayed in getting to the trailhead and got a late start on our hike. It was late fall, so the sun would set pretty early (and you lose light faster in the mountains), and there was a very early cold front coming in with temperatures that were expected to get into the high single digits. However, I knew that with the distance we had to go, if we kept a good pace we would make it to camp with enough daylight left to set up camp and build the fire we would need in the cold.

The problem came after we had been hiking for a good while, and I noticed the trail was no longer heading in the direction that was shown on the map. I realized we had wandered quite a way off the correct path. The problem was that if we backtracked to get to the original trail and followed it to the campsite, we wouldn't arrive into camp until after sunset. That meant risking a hike in the dark and getting lost again. And if we made it to camp after sunset, it would be difficult to create a fire in the dark, and we would be at risk of not being able to cook our dinner.

So at this point we had three choices. First, as I just outlined, we could backtrack, follow the trail, risk getting lost, and plan on getting to camp in the dark. The second option was to go off trail and attempt to take a direct route to the camp utilizing our navigation skills. The upside to this was that the direct route should be faster and gave us the possibility of getting to camp before dark. The downside was that we didn't know how rough the terrain would be. If it was really rough it might be slower, and then we would get to camp even later, or worse, risk hiking in the dark without a trail and increasing our chances of getting lost. The third option was to abandon the camping trip and just follow the trail all the way back to the truck. We would arrive at the truck after dark, but then we could just drive home where we were guaranteed a warm bed and a meal.

Faced with this decision, asking myself, "What is the right thing to do?" was not helpful. This was not a choice of right and wrong. What I needed in that moment was not a moral compass to help me choose right. What I needed was wisdom.

Unfortunately, wisdom is not a word we hear very often any more. How often have you heard anyone on television or in popular culture use the word wisdom? Rarely, I would guess.

But hopefully you have someone in your life who you consider to be wise. You may not consciously say that person has "wisdom," but they are the person you call when you need advice or to help you think through an issue. Why do you call that person and not someone else? You may say they have good judgment. They have strong insights. Maybe they have knowledge of a certain area and a unique understanding that comes from that knowledge. Perhaps it is because you hope to learn something from their experiences.

Wisdom is one of those things that is difficult to define, and yet we recognize it when we encounter it.

Wisdom necessarily involves taking long-term ramifications into consideration—how this decision will impact the future. It involves considering consequences—thinking through what may happen as a result of this action. Wisdom is the ability to take all of these things—knowledge, experience, understanding, insight—and use good judgment to best apply them to making a decision or choosing an action that will lead to the most desirous outcome over time.

Therefore, to be wise you must know what is desirous. Wisdom is a vehicle to manipulate your life circumstances to create a reality that most closely resembles your image of your ideal state of being. Your ideal state of being is what you call success, and success for you is determined by your emotional drivers and values.

Pastor Andy Stanley coined a brilliant question to help understand what wisdom is and how it should best drive our decision making. He says that when you are faced with a decision, ask yourself, "In light of my past experiences, my current circumstances, and my future hopes and dreams, what is the wise thing for me to do?" If wisdom can be learned, using this question seems like a good way to learn it.

If you can't remember all of that, here is a shorter version: "Ten years from now, what will I wish I had done?" The idea is to think of your future self looking back on this decision and evaluating if you made the right choice. This question forces you to think about long-term consequences, how you hope to exist in the future, and how this decision will impact that existence.

When I was in the cold woods with my son, I needed to use wisdom to make a choice about which route to take. Following Pastor Stanley's question, first I had to consider my past experiences in this area. I knew that hiking in the dark was hard; I'd done it before. It is easy to get lost. I have spent time outdoors in severe cold, and I knew that your mind tends to slow down, leading to bad decisions. I had to consider that risk. I also knew that hiking off-trail becomes very difficult. The woods in the North Georgia mountains are full of thickets and other things that make it difficult to walk, and the rough terrain covered in loose dead leaves makes slipping very common. Finally, I realized that as a grown adult and experienced hiker, I could probably overcome these off-trail obstacles, but a tired, cold 10-year-old boy would probably struggle quickly.

However, the insights I had from experience also told me that if the worst came, and we were lost in the woods as the severe cold crept in, we had the gear to survive. Even if we couldn't cook our food, we had enough cold rations to be able to sustain us until the morning when we could more easily find our way. We could connect our sleeping bags and even use our combined body heat to survive the night if necessary. As tough as it might be, I knew we would be okay.

So, what were my "future hopes and dreams" in relation to this situation? What values informed my definition of success for this trip? Certainly, I value the safety of my child. Part of my job as a parent is to protect him. It was a given that I would not do anything that created an unacceptable level of risk of physical harm. I also value the precious one-on-one time that we get, so abandoning the trip was unattractive. But more than anything, I considered why I take my kids on backpacking trips. Partially these trips are designed to help them appreciate the magnificence of nature and help them realize the beauty that surrounds them. The trips increase gratitude by forcing them to work at things such as purifying water or gathering wood to burn for cooking and warmth—things we have come to take for granted. But mostly, I want them to have adventures that build confidence by allowing them to overcome challenges and creatively solve problems when things aren't easy or comfortable. This value is what most drove my definition of success for the trip.

My guess is that this story resembles many decisions that you are faced with. Not decisions of right and wrong, but decisions where some of your values seem to conflict and you are unsure about the best path to take. The more responsibility you have, the more people you lead, the more resources you oversee, the more complex and the less clear these decisions become. It is for these times we need wisdom.

We make business decisions daily that call for wisdom. It seems like so many of them revolve around people. Should I insist on a deadline that the team thinks will be hard to hit? Should I confront my boss with something I think she did wrong? Which customer's order should I work on first? Should I promote that salesperson to manager?

These are not questions of right and wrong. Sometimes giving teams lofty goals brings out the best in them, and sometimes it demoralizes them. Sometimes confronting a person directly brings the best outcome, and sometimes it is better to go with an intermediary. One customer may have a more lucrative order, but may not take priority over a customer that has been more valuable over the long term. And discerning if a salesperson will be successful as a sales manager requires Solomon-esque levels of wisdom.

So what did I do that evening in the woods? Well, I decided on what was somewhat of a fourth option. I believed that by taking a shortcut over a ridge we could reconnect with the trail. It was longer than the direct route but less risky. If it didn't work, we had a good chance of at least finding the trail before dark so we could bed down and then find our way in the morning. Turns out it did work and we rolled into camp at dusk. We had enough light to find some firewood and get our fire going before the temperature got too cold. We had a late dinner and had to setup a tent in the dark, but we were warm and full when we went to bed.

Someone else would have probably made a different decision. Someone with less experience in the woods or someone who values safety above all else might have used their best judgment and headed back to the truck. But in my judgment, the upside of the lessons learned by that 10-year-old boy were worth more than the discomfort of a cold night on the side of a mountain.

And years later, he still brings up that trip all the time.

Does Wisdom = Integrity?

We commonly think of wise people as being virtuous, of understanding right from wrong. I doubt you've ever thought of someone with low integrity as wise. People who are wise, who are able to consider the long term, who are able to think through the ramifications of decisions on many people and across much time— these people settle on virtues such as integrity and honesty because these are the values that drive decisions that lead to the most exceptional forms of success. Indeed, wisdom does not merely derive from virtues such as these, it leads to them.

So those who are honest are not necessarily wise, but those who are wise are honest. Wise people act with integrity because over the long term, integrity often lends itself to both economic riches and rich relationships. Wise people serve others because they know it yields mental and physical well-being that far surpasses what can be achieved through any other means.

My definition of wisdom is "the discernment to determine the best methods to achieve the best objectives." It takes wisdom to know which action to take to achieve a goal, but it also takes wisdom to determine which goals are worth achieving.

14
Keep Getting Better

For ten years I competed in triathlons. I never won a race, but every year, I set goals to get faster or place better, and I worked relentlessly toward those goals.

If you are going to take the sport of triathlon even semi-seriously, you have to be prepared to commit a hefty amount of time and make sacrifices in other areas of your life. Your body is often going to be physically tired, and you will occasionally suffer injuries. In the three to four months leading up to my "A" races, I worked out nine times a week, with most of those workouts coming before sunrise because I had young kids to raise and a company to lead.

Let me tell you that if I did not have highly motivating, public goals, I would have chosen most mornings to ignore the 4:45 alarm clock and go back to sleep. However, I fell in love with the results of what that discipline did in my life. The physical, mental, and spiritual rewards were immense. The races were just a celebration of what the training achieved in my life and a way to mark progress along the journey. It was the expectation that I put on myself to keep improving that yielded the benefits.

Organizations function in the same way. When they set lofty goals that force them to stretch, they make better decisions. They put in place the disciplines that force them to do better and be better.

Even if this value doesn't seem natural to you, I believe there is both an economic and moral imperative for growth.

Let's say you have a choice of investing in two companies. One is a company that is in decline and earning less with each passing year. The other is growing and earning more and more. Which would you choose? Okay, that's a dumb question. Of course you would choose the growing company. You have an asset of value (cash), and you don't want to waste it in an investment that is going to cause that value to decline. Further, you know that the cash will help you achieve other things of value to you (such as sending your kids to college), and you want to utilize it in the best way you can to achieve that long-term, highly desirous goal of providing for your child's education.

If a company is not getting a proper return on its assets, the owners, employees, and other stakeholders will demand that it change course, or it will cease to exist. It will either close down or someone will buy it who is better able to maximize the value of its assets. People will not maintain their investments in assets that are underperforming, or not "living up to their potential." This is the economic imperative for growth—if a business isn't growing, it is dying.

All resources are able to generate some value for someone. If a resource or asset is wasted, that means that someone is not able to satisfy their physical or emotional needs to their fullest. This is true for people too. And it includes you.

Let's take a couple examples to see how this applies to you as an individual.

Think about your spouse or closest friend. Is there anything they could do to improve as a partner or friend? Is there something new they could do that would make the relationship richer? Is there something they are doing that they need to eliminate because it is hurting the relationship?

What if I asked this question to them about you?

Think about your parents. Is there something they could have done differently that would have impacted your life in a positive way? Perhaps if they had learned to discipline you differently, might that have changed some of your negative behaviors later in life?

What is the possibility that you could learn something that might make you a better parent to your child?

When you think about other people in your life, you can see how their stagnation may have impacted you. If they had kept growing in the knowledge about parenting or their ability to communicate, you would have experienced the difference. And of course, the same could be said about you. This is the moral imperative for growth.

But the argument for growth is not just about your impact on other people. It's about your intrinsic rewards for a life well lived.

Consider the joy you get from different aspects of your life. Before I started doing triathlons, I hardly knew how to swim. The growth I experienced as an athlete led to a decade of doing something I loved. Yes, it reaped all kinds of rewards in the form of life lessons that I can share with others, but it was also just a joy to do. Had I not put in the effort to learn to swim, I would have missed out on that. It fills me with wonder to consider what other joy-filled experiences await me as I continue to push myself to do new things as a part of a journey of growth.

I also love to read. Sometimes I read what I call "brain-dead fiction" just for fun on vacation, but what I really enjoy is reading history, philosophy or psychology, and classic literature. I love reading something that gives me new perspective on people or events. I always feel more empowered as I gain a better understanding of the world and how it works. As a result, I make better decisions and am better able to influence people.

Now, I suppose one could argue that only those who are discontent feel the need to grow. If you are content with what you have and who you are, there is nothing driving a desire to change your circumstances, your knowledge, or experiences. I would argue that contentment and growth are not necessarily opposing ideals—one can be both content and desirous of improving oneself.

Growth is rewarding unto itself. To not grow means waste. Waste is punished in the market, but a wasted life is even sadder to contemplate.

Here are a few principles of growth that I learned from my dad:

No Growth Without Failure

If you are growing, you are going to have failures. In fact, I would argue that growth necessarily involves failure. We improve by failing and then learning from our failure.

One of the descriptors we often hear when people explain the culture of our company is "risk-free environment." What this means is that people are free from the consequences of failure because we know that you have to take risks (the risk of failing) if you are going to grow. We don't punish failure as long as you learn from it—grow from it.

Take Personal Responsibility

You will never learn if every problem is always someone else's fault. You are in charge of your life. In every situation there is something different you could have done to improve the outcome—even if it is just owning your own reaction or emotional state. If you are always the victim of circumstance or of other people's actions, there is no opportunity for you to improve or grow.

As a manager, if someone on your team misses their goals, whose fault is it? Theirs? Well, yes. But isn't it also yours? Did you do a perfect job training them? Did you provide them with perfectly timed communication? Even if the answers to these two questions are (amazingly) yes, then did you hire the wrong person?

People who are growing know that sometimes they will fail, and when they do so, they own their part of the failure. That way, they are able to analyze what happened and learn from it, so they are better prepared for situations in the future. They grow.

Be the Best

You may or may not achieve being the best at something, but if you set being the best as your goal, it will force you to figure out what it takes to become the best. And at a minimum, those actions are going to make you better. Setting the expectation that you are going to be the best creates a picture that you (and those on your team) will strive to live up to.

You have no doubt seen it on countless pictures of cats: "Success is a journey, not a destination." The posters may be silly but the sentiment is true—great visions have the quality of never being quite finished. The only sad part of a triathlon was always about an hour after I was done. All that work and effort peaked as I crossed the finish line, leaving a sense of "Now what?"

It is the vision of each Jackson Healthcare company to be the "premier" or "unparalleled" company in its niche. These are not static positions. Once you become the best, other businesses copy what you do, and you have to keep getting better or lose your position. Today's record is tomorrow's second place. But seeking to be the best you can be at all times—that is a tremendous journey.

Beliefs

Beliefs are convictions that something is true, good, right, or valuable. They come to be through personal and group experiences, and they, along with values, shape our decisions. If a member of a group has different beliefs from the group at large (especially strong beliefs that he or she will defend at great cost), then that member will stick out and will ultimately leave voluntarily or be asked to leave by the group.

Therefore, we think it is important that members (and especially leaders) of our company understand our closely held beliefs in regards to running a business. Some of these beliefs originated with my father, some grew out of my own experiences, and many have developed with the help of our senior leadership and some outside influences. While there are certainly different ways to apply these beliefs, we seek consistency in using them as a framework for decision-making. We keep these beliefs at the forefront as we seek to achieve our vision and mission, which reflect our definition of success.

You won't be surprised to hear that we have many beliefs about how the business should run. I have tried to include here only the major ones—those we feel most strongly about and are high on the continuum of defense. For purposes of organization, I have divided these beliefs into four categories based on how they are most often applied in business: Organizational, Operational, Managerial, and Relational.

Organizational Beliefs

For the purpose of this topic, organizational beliefs are those that apply to how one thinks about the business at a high level—about the organization as a whole. The fact that we have a set of beliefs about how to think about the organization tells you something in itself. It is important to make sure you are thinking about the big picture—about the company itself—and not just what it does.

15
Working on the Business

In *The 4 Disciplines of Execution*, Chris McChesney calls it "the whirlwind." I call it "the tornado," but we are talking about the same thing. It is the busy-ness of day-to-day business activity that just sucks you in. The unending emails that need a response, calls to make, reports to read, or meetings to attend. We both hate the tornado and love the tornado. We hate the tornado because it is never-ending and makes it difficult to see progress. We love it because it is easy—easy to know what to do and feel like we accomplished something every time we check another menial task off the to-do list.

Don't get me wrong—the tornado exists for a reason. Indeed, those things must get done so that customers are serviced, revenue is generated, and people get paid. But when you are inside the tornado, you can't see where it is going or the damage it is doing. You just go around and around.

My dad calls it working *in* the business. Yes, you must work in the business. In fact, understanding the details of the business by gaining firsthand knowledge is incredibly valuable. But occasionally (and more often, if possible), you must pull yourself out to work *on* the business.

Working on the business is strategy. It is asking the question, "Are we doing the right things?" and not just, "Are we doing things right?" It is making sure that we truly understand the problems we are solving for our customers. It is forcing ourselves to innovate and improve. Working on the business means that we continually figure out how to be different and how to be known for that difference. It means assuring that everyone working in the business knows how we define success and how they contribute to that success. It is solving issues before they become problems and making sure that our associates win when the company wins.

Working on the business recognizes that the business is a thing unto itself. The business is a product that results from our purposeful creation, or alternatively, it is the default result of our subconscious neglect. Like the engine of a car, the business is a mechanism that exists to solve a problem, provide a service, and do a job. And like an engine, if it is not serviced, maintained, and improved, it will fail and become obsolete.

We ask our leaders to go through strategic planning and other exercises aimed at forcing opportunities to work on the business. This is designed to help them overcome the overwhelming pull of the tornado. But all of us must keep this principle in mind, whether we are running a business or running our lives. Improvement happens when we are able to take a step back and think about how to improve.

Triathlons start with open-water swims. In addition to the sheer physical effort it takes to swim that far in a river, lake, or ocean, added difficulty comes from trying to figure out which direction to go. Swim training happens in a pool where you follow a visible line on the bottom that takes you to the other end. In open water, that line doesn't exist. You can easily spot the rookies in a triathlon because they're swimming all over the lake and nowhere near the direction of the finish line. More experienced open-water swimmers have learned to "sight"—an act where you pause your stroke motion to put your head up and find where you are so you can redirect your path toward the finish line. Rookies don't know to do this. They swim like they do in the pool—continually stroking as hard as they can without stopping to look up. They are in a race and don't want to pause even for a moment for fear of getting behind. Pretty soon they are way off course, and when they finally look up, they have to swim twice as far as they would have had they taken the time to sight correctly.

In business and in life we can swim and swim, stroking hard and efficiently, but if we don't occasionally look up to make sure we are on the right course, we are going to wind up working hard and missing the finish line.

16
Focus and Specialization

This belief probably impacts the way we structure and operate our businesses more than any other. We believe strongly in the power of focus and specialization. When you specialize in something, you become the expert. On the contrary, a generalist is mediocre at many things but great at nothing.

People want the best (at least the best they can afford). When given a choice between two products of the same kind but differing quality, which would you choose? The better one of course. When you are buying a service, you want to deal with the expert. If you need heart surgery, who would you rather perform the procedure—a cardiac surgeon or a general surgeon?

There are some unique people who are able to be really good at a number of things, but they are rare indeed. During my lifetime, I have seen two people who were able to play multiple professional sports at the highest level. Bo Jackson and Deion Sanders both played in the NFL and Major League Baseball. Think about that. Of all the thousands of people who have played professional sports over the past few decades, out of all the amazing athletes, there are only two who have been able to play more than one. Even the great Michael Jordan couldn't make it out of the minor leagues when he tried to play baseball. To compete at the highest levels, athletes must focus. And not just on one sport, but on one position in that sport.

For most of us mere mortals, we don't have the raw skill to develop expertise in multiple areas. If we are going to be good at something, we have to dedicate the time necessary to develop that skill. So needless to say, the smaller the scope of the task or skill, the easier it is to become good at it.

This belief has so many applications—it is astounding.

If there are 100 steps in executing a solution for a client, how many people are there in the world who are absolute experts in all 100 steps? If you are creating a software technology, how many people are there who can create the code, database, user interface, performance specifications, testing scenarios, and implementation procedures? I'm sure a few people could do all of that, but how would their product compare to something created by a group of people, each of whom was an expert in their individual area?

We are always looking for ways to narrow the scope and increase the focus of people's jobs in an effort to enable them to become an expert at that job. The generalist can't compete against the specialist on quality, but they also can't scale their business. Let's say you do find the Bo Jackson of your industry—someone who can do it all—how many more Bo Jacksons are out there to hire? I'll give you your one Bo Jackson, and I'll hire a bunch of linemen, running backs, and quarterbacks who are plentiful and enter the draft in droves. By the time you hire your second person, I'll have already won the Super Bowl.

This concept applies not just at the individual level, but at the organizational level. We look to focus teams as much as possible. In our business line of temporary physician staffing, we are always looking to create a narrower focus for each team. We don't just offer clients a group of people who are experts in the process of staffing a physician, we provide them with a team of experts in the process of placing a surgeon. What's more, our clients are actually dealing with a team of people who are experts at placing a surgeon in their part of their state.

For our salespeople and producers, we are continually trying to have them focus on smaller and smaller territories. Now, this is counterintuitive to a salesperson and is typically met with some resistance at first, but almost every time we reduce someone's territory, they earn more commissions the next year. The example I give people that are going through a territory change is this:

Let's say that I took our best recruiter and told him that he could only place psychiatrists in our hometown of Alpharetta, GA. Alpharetta is a suburb of Atlanta with a population of about 65,000. With such a focused territory, that recruiter would probably know every psychiatrist in Alpharetta, not to mention the names of their family members, when they are available to work, what kind of patients they are qualified to see, and probably whether they like cream in their coffee! There would literally be no one more qualified in the world to place psychiatrists in Alpharetta than that recruiter. They would be the undisputed expert. Imagine them competing with someone who places any doctor anywhere in the country. Who will be quicker to market with superior candidates?

In a service business, creating differentiation is difficult. Focus yields the opportunity to create differentiation. When you specialize, you understand the problems of your customers better and become the expert they need in solving those problems.

But this concept doesn't just apply to the individual or organizational structure. We seek to be specialized as a business strategy. All of our companies are built to create business models that enable them to become the experts in solving a particular problem for a customer. The whole business is specialized.

In staffing, we are often competing against people who staff many types of positions for many types of customers. Perhaps they are focused on an industry such as healthcare. One of our companies consists of a team who thinks about nothing but how to put nurses to work where they are needed most. That's it. Who do you think will be better at placing nurses—them or the generalist?

Now the "art" in specialization is to determine if the level of specialization is addressing a problem that is big enough to justify the dedication to that specialty. This is true at the task, job, team, or company level. I could create a job for someone to do nothing but staple papers in our office, but there simply isn't enough demand for stapling papers to justify that position. Whether we are creating a role on a team, a territory for a salesperson, a team that focuses on one service, or even creating a new business, we are looking for the most focused problem we can solve in a market that is big enough to sustain that job, salesperson, team, or company. This results in businesses that create unique value for their customers and can scale quickly.

A skeptic might say that this minute focus would result in a bunch of boring jobs. It might sound like working on a factory line where all you do is put the same bolt on the same kind of cars all day. Certainly, there is a danger of that if you don't create the jobs the right way. But we have found that people enjoy being really good at something. Often the more of an expert someone becomes in their area, the more they understand the problem they are solving, and they see how much better they can become. Plus, these levels of expertise enable them to begin applying that expertise into other related fields.

It can be difficult to discern the right level of specialization. How does one know if a different service line is adjacent to what they do and should be grafted in, or a distraction that should be avoided? One must constantly evaluate their scope of activities to determine if they are solving a big enough and specific enough problem for their customer.

Specialization is a belief that applies at every level of our companies. It is the filter through which we see everything from our business strategy to the everyday task. Our companies lead the market because we have focused in a way that makes them the best at solving worthy problems for their customers. And our operations are second to none because we create an environment where people can become experts in how they perform their jobs.

But other than that, it's really not that important...

17
Define Success

One of the quickest ways to determine what you really value is to ask yourself this question: "What is my definition of success?" The answer will reveal your values, and as we discussed earlier, those values will in large part determine how you make decisions. The same is true for a business. How an organization defines success will determine the decisions it makes—how it operates, how it handles customers, and how it treats people.

One of my favorite movie dialogs is from Disney's 1951 classic *Alice in Wonderland* when Alice meets the Cheshire Cat (which incidentally is way better than the same scene in the book).

> *Alice: Thank you, but I just wanted to ask you which way I ought to go.*
> *Cheshire Cat: Well, that depends on where you want to get to.*
> *Alice: Oh, it really doesn't matter, as long as I can...*
> *Cheshire Cat: Then it really doesn't matter which way you go!*

If you don't know where you want to "get to," then when faced with diverging paths, it doesn't matter which way you go. Said differently, if you don't know what you are trying to accomplish, then how do you know what decision to make?

Every person in your organization or on your team is faced with numerous decisions daily. Which customer do I call first? Which task do I prioritize and which do I neglect? How do I handle this situation? As a leader, one of your primary responsibilities is to make sure the people on your team know how to answer those questions. Your job is to make sure they know what we are trying to accomplish (our definition of success) and how their jobs help us accomplish that.

In every organization that I have led, the first thing I've done is clearly articulate our vision and mission. In this context, my definition of vision is what we are trying to accomplish as a business, and mission is why we are trying to accomplish it. Vision is "what," and mission is "so what?" They combine to answer the question of how we define success.

If there is a lack of clarity about the group's definition of success, then each group member will create a defnition based on their personal goals and view of the group's aims. Eventually they will probably figure out what the group's true objectives are based on seeing how people act (deciphering the culture), but they may do a lot of damage in the meantime by acting against what the company is trying to accomplish.

Unfortunately, this dictum comes with a warning. When you talk about your vision and mission—what you are trying to accomplish and why—it creates vulnerability for you as a leader. It is now time to put up or shut up. If you say that your vision is one thing, but your actions reveal that you are actually pursuing something else, then people will see your hypocrisy very quickly, and you will lose credibility with them.

However, if you are able to clearly articulate success and attract other people who define success the same way, then you will create something incredibly powerful. Training is easier, communication is faster, and customers experience consistency.

It is amazing how fast a boat can go when all oars are rowing to the same rhythm. Everything goes faster because everyone knows where you are going.

18
Create a Picture

I love inspirational quotes. They elevate your thinking, give you hope, or raise your level of awareness. However, some of them are just too hokey and are irritating even to me. One of them is often attributed to Walt Disney: "If you can dream it, you can do it!"

Really? I have dreamed of flying like Superman since I was a little boy, and somehow, I still can't do it.

However silly this quote is, I do think there is value in creating aspirational goals. We put limits on our self in the form of assumptions about what we can and cannot do. We create pictures of ourselves (how we act, what we are good at, and what we are not), and then we live up to that picture.

People subconsciously manipulate their behavior and environments to make their reality match their picture of reality. If you say, "I always end up in relationships with cruel people," guess who you will choose to date? "I always end up in dead end jobs." Guess what kind of job you will take? "I can't ever close the big deal." Guess who tanks the sales call?

But what if your picture changed?

What if the person who believed that they weren't good at public speaking somehow adopted a new picture of themselves in which they are a good public speaker? Do you think they could change behaviors to fulfill that picture?

It is not easy, but I believe this can be done. Unfortunately, it is not as easy as dreaming it and then doing it.

It starts with creating a new, attractive picture. You must then regularly and continually focus on that picture so that through repetition, you can begin to replace the old picture. Then you must seek reasons to believe that the picture is, in fact, possible and even probable[3].

This can be done in people as well as in organizations. As a leader, it is not enough to set a vision of some grandiose state in the future. More than likely, your vision is going to be different from other people's views of the current situation, and their immediate reaction will be to reject it. To create belief in the vision, you must regularly reinforce it with reasons that will help people understand why they should believe it will be true.

When I started at LocumTenens.com, I stated the vision that we were going to be the industry's premier provider of locum tenens services in market share, profitability, customer satisfaction, associate satisfaction, and quality. At that time, we were way down the list in industry market share. We had started several years after the industry leaders and were largely unknown relative to them. I got a lot of skeptical looks and

---

[3] There is a lot of psychological theory behind this concept that I am summarizing incredibly quickly. For several years, we have taught a class at Jackson Healthcare University called "Achieving Your Potential" that discusses these concepts in depth and how to apply them at a personal level. For more, you can also read Lou Tice's *Smart Talk For Achieving Your Potential: 5 Steps to Get You From Here to There.*

comments when I started speaking about this vision. However, I just kept repeating it over and over in any situation I could. I continually pointed out all the things we were doing that were going to make us the market leader. Eventually, the evidence I presented was so overwhelming that people believed it, and it became accepted that it was just a matter of time before we surpassed everyone else.

But the important thing is that once people started believing that we were the best, they started acting like it. Our people pictured our organization as the best in the business at taking care of our customers, so when a problem came up with a customer, they would react like someone who is the best would react. Our picture showed that we would grow organically every year by at least 50% more than the market as a whole, so guess what we did? We manipulated our behavior to fulfill that picture.

It is easy to dream up aspirational goals. A leader's job is to create a picture of who we are so that we all live up to making that picture reality.

Shine a Light on Desired Behavior

One of the best ways to create a picture is to highlight and reward desired behavior. I am a big fan of giving awards and recognition and believe that even people who claim not to care about recognition secretly do. However, it is worthless to give someone an award if they don't know what it's for.

One of our companies was in the habit of giving out an award for the Associate of the Month. One month, the leader of the company realized that they had forgotten to announce the award for the past few months. She quickly sent out an email with the names of the people who had won for the past five months. There was no explanation of what each had done to win.

I asked her what the point was of giving out the award.

"Well, they each got a $100 gift card."

"So, do they know what they would need to do to win that gift card again?"

No. They might as well have had a random drawing. The company got no benefit from spending that money, and the people got no satisfaction for having done something worthy of recognition.

When we give awards, we must give detailed descriptions of the behavior that led to the award. It not only lets the winner know what they need to do to win again, but it shows everyone else what they need to do to get recognized.

But you don't have to give away an award, and there doesn't have to be money attached. Publicly praise someone for the kind of behavior you want to see, and you will start seeing more of it from them and others.

19
The Plan is Nothing; Planning is Everything

Wouldn't it be wonderful if nothing ever changed, and everything we think we know is correct? What if we had perfect knowledge about people and markets, and we could create processes right the first time? Talk about Wonderland—I don't think even the Mad Hatter would believe this place exists!

The challenge is that we often run our businesses like the statements above are true. We create business plans assuming we know everything about the market, exactly what the solutions are to the market problem we want to solve, and exactly how our people and processes will act in delivering those solutions. Then we take this plan and put it on a shelf to collect dust until perhaps we pull it out to reference in next year's plan.

I have written a lot of business plans over the years. I've created many, many financial forecasts. There was one thing that was consistent about all of them:

They were all wrong.

Not wrong because I am dumb or reached bad conclusions or had stupid ideas. They were wrong because the information I had when creating the plan was limited and sometimes incorrect. Because I had hypotheses about how the market would react but not proof. Because I made an assumption that the way a small group of customers behaved was representative of the way the rest of the market would behave. Because I thought I could hire people with certain skills at a specific time but had not yet done so.

There is an old adage that no battle plan survives contact with the enemy. Much the same could be said for business plans.

So does that mean that we shouldn't write business plans? Certainly not! What it means is that they should be living documents that are constantly scrutinized, challenged, and refined as we get more and better information.

The most important part of writing a business plan is the process, not the plan itself. The questions one attempts to answer in strategic planning—who is our customer, what are their needs, how do we deliver, etc.—should be asked and answered often.

One of the most important parts of our strategic planning process is identifying assumptions. What are the things you think you know that drive how you create this plan? There is incredible value in knowing what your assumptions are so that you can test them and either turn them into facts or change them altogether. Your assumptions drive your business solution and business model—what problem you are trying to solve in the market and how you deliver that solution. If you don't know what they are, it takes much longer to figure out what is and isn't working.

The message here for leaders is that you need to build a rhythm of learning in your organization. Make sure that you are regularly "working on the business" in a way that has you identifying and challenging the assumptions behind your business. What has changed in the market? Or in our ability to deliver? We built this plan thinking one thing, but then discovered that something else actually happened. Now how do we react?

Focus on the process of planning, and the plan will get much better.

20
Build for Legacy

Legacy is something that is transmitted by or received from a predecessor or ancestor. The word's origin regards gifts of money or personal property in a will when someone dies, but its meaning has grown to encompass much more than that. For instance, one could say that the systems of government and law in today's Western civilization are the legacy of ancient Greece. The philosophies they created that were later revived in the Enlightenment were the basis for how most Western governments were formed.

On a personal level, it is a humbling but valuable exercise to consider the legacy you will leave. All of us have the potential to live in such a way that impacts others—for better or worse.

Similar to defining success, this exercise forces you to think long term and reveals your values. But unlike defining success, articulating the legacy you hope to leave involves solely considering your impact on others. Your legacy is enjoyed or suffered by other people.

Or is it?

I think it is appropriate and helpful to also consider the legacy you leave to your later self. How will you as someone 15 years older than you are now look back on today's version of you? Will you regret decisions you made that have had negative consequences? Will the current you leave your future self with rich relationships or loneliness? Will your legacy be filled with fond memories or despair over time wasted?

The mission of Jackson Healthcare is to improve the delivery of patient care and the lives of everyone we touch. The second part—improving the lives of everyone we touch—has become the mantra for our company. It summarizes the legacy we want to leave. Our desire is that everyone with whom we come into contact is better because of that interaction. We want to leave a legacy with our customers, associates, vendors, and communities of helping people improve their lives. The desire for that legacy is why we exist as a company.

To do this, we must not only consider how we operate the company today, but we must also consider how to structure the company for sustainability in the future. We want Jackson Healthcare to be an engine that serves other people for many years to come.

This long-term thinking impacts everything we do, and I think it has been one of the keys to our success. It changes the way we interact with customers. When you believe that you are going to be working with a customer for the next 10 years, it changes the way you approach them today. Many if not most people view their job as a short-term stop on the way to something else. Many people who start or run a business are doing so with the short-term goal of selling the company to someone else. They have no thought of the legacy they are leaving themselves (nor anyone else) in the business, as they don't believe that they will be in the business for the long term.

So when someone in our company is competing against someone in another company, the customer is offered two different experiences—one involving someone whose goal is to maximize short-term value and the other whose goal is to maximize long-term value. The first offers a transaction, the second, a relationship.

Occasionally, I get entrepreneurs asking me what they should do to position their company to sell. I tell them that they should run their company as if they are never going to sell, as this will create more value whether they decide to sell or not. They typically look at me funny and immediately dismiss what I say.

If you wait until the end of your life to consider what you want your legacy to be, it will be too late to do anything about it. Your legacy will be largely determined by then. Every action you take today is creating the legacy you will leave to others and to your future self. Decide what that legacy will be and then take purposeful action today to assure you succeed in leaving the legacy you desire.

Operational Beliefs

This section lays out some of our more ardent beliefs about operating a business. It is a blurry line between categories, and some of these could also be viewed as organizational or managerial philosophies. But the overarching theme of the beliefs in this section is how they apply to running a business or team.

21
Efficiency vs. Effectiveness

Here is a summary of a fable I have probably heard my dad tell a hundred times:

A man wants to catch fish, so he goes to the fishing store and buys all of the latest gear. He gets the best rod and reel, the most attractive lures and bait, and the sleekest boat with the quietest motor. He has all the tackle you would ever need. He even takes fishing lessons from a professional to learn the most effective techniques for casting and setting the hook in various kinds of fish. He heads out to the lake ready to catch fish.

A second man goes out to fish in a different lake. He doesn't really know much about fishing, but he takes an old rod and reel with a lure he found in the garage. He doesn't have a fancy boat, but finds an old jon boat that he takes out onto the lake.

The second man catches fish after fish. The first man catches nothing.

What happened?

Now you may be thinking of all kinds of morals that could come from this. Something about a connection with nature or overanalyzing things, or how commercialization ruins simple pleasures. No, this isn't that fancy of a fable. The punch line is simply this: the second man was on a lake with lots of fish. The first man was on a lake with no fish.

My dad calls this, "Doing things right versus doing the right thing." It doesn't matter how good of a fisherman you are if you are on a lake with no fish. You can do everything right, but if you aren't doing the right thing, it doesn't matter.

The strategic implication of this fable is that it doesn't matter how well you execute if you are selling a product no one wants. It's better to be mediocre at selling a product with lots of demand than excellent at selling something with no demand. Spend more time figuring out where the fish are and less time worrying about what color the boat should be.

For businesses that are, in fact, operating on a lake with fish in it, I see this principle playing out in what I call the battle between efficiency and effectiveness.

I am all for efficiency—figuring out how to do more with less. Efficiency can make people more productive, and ultimately, increase profit margins. These are both good things, but I am much more interested in effectiveness than I am efficiency. Who wants to be efficient at something that is ineffective? Give me a wasteful yet effective solution over an efficient but ineffective one any day. Do the right thing before figuring out how to do it right.

If you are a manager in a business with any kind of scale, my guess is that you see this all the time. We focus so much on automation and standardization, but the net result of these efforts often has nothing to do with effectively delivering service to our customers. Even worse, sometimes we make decisions in the name of efficiency that actually make it harder to deliver for our customers.

My most memorable example of this was a time when my accounting department wanted to change a process so they could handle it more efficiently. It was a great presentation that stated the problem they were having and how, by standardizing the process, they wouldn't have to add headcount to their team to handle rising volume, thus increasing profitability of the company in the future. Clear ROI. The problem was that the process they wanted to standardize was something that directly impacted our customers—something our customers depended on for flexibility. This flexibility was a big part of the value we offered our customers. So my response was that it would be great to execute this process more efficiently, but by doing so, we would lose our customers—without whom we would have no need for the process at all! I will gladly put up with inefficiency if it yields effectiveness.

One time our company was up for a quality award. To qualify we had to endure a multiple-day audit of our entire business by a panel of judges. I met with one of the judges at the end, and he started by giving me a lecture about how we need to do a better job of documenting processes on one of our teams that had four (yes, four) people. He went on and on about how it would make us more efficient at onboarding new people and enable us to do process analysis. Being able to take no more, I retorted that this was a new team that was trying to create a new service line for us. By the time they documented a process, they would have figured out that it needed to change. Plus, with such a small team, there was no practical use for such documentation—the speed of communication is instant and new people learn by observing their teammates. Not to mention that in the time it would take to document all their processes, they would probably go out of business because they wouldn't have any time to sell business or service customers!

We didn't win the award.

But that team is now a multimillion-dollar division. So I think I won the argument after all.

Of course, the answer is that you want to be both efficient and effective—do the right thing and do it right. The problem is that organizations have the gravitational pull towards ineffective but efficient processes, which leaders have to constantly battle.

If you can achieve efficiency and effectiveness, by all means, do it. But when given the choice, keep your business strategy in mind, and choose how you can most effectively deliver it.

Who Knows You

We all know the old adage that it's not what you know but who you know. There are certainly many occasions where knowing the right person makes all the difference. Knowing the person who can put in a good word or get you in the door can mean securing the meeting or getting out of the ticket. But there is something even more powerful than having a big network. Even better than knowing lots of people.

It's having lots of people know you.

For several years we have had two physician staffing companies who compete against each other: one we started and one we bought. Shortly after we purchased the second company, two recruiters were talking to each other about their jobs. Each recruited the same specialty physician. One was complaining about all the time he had to spend "cold calling" doctors to see if they were interested in the work opportunities he had. He asked his counterpart if he also got tired of cold calling.

"I don't know," he answered. "I don't really do any cold calling."

"Then how do you find the doctors?" he asked.

"They call me. I just answer the phone."

That is the result of effective marketing. The one recruiter was certainly doing things right by making cold calls, but by doing the right things, the marketing department at the other company was helping their recruiter to be far more effective.

22
Fail Fast and Often

Winston Churchill is credited with saying, "Success consists of going from failure to failure without loss of enthusiasm." I love the name of Joey Green's book, *The Road to Success is Paved with Failure*. Thomas Edison failed thousands of times before successfully inventing the light bulb. Michael Jordan missed thousands of shots. Whoever you want to cite or quote, it is clear that success comes with and after many failures.

So, to speed up on the road to success, should you just try to fail on purpose?

Well, yeah, sort of.

In Chapter 19, we discussed how the process of planning is more important than the plan itself because you are constantly learning and gathering new information that informs and potentially alters your business plan. The key point is that you are always learning and incorporating the lessons learned into your strategy. This same principle applies to operating your business, particularly when it comes to innovation.

Newton's first law of motion states, "Every object persists in its state of rest or uniform motion in a straight line unless it is compelled to change that state by forces impressed on it." I would submit that this applies not just to objects in space, but also to people and groups.

Most people do not seek change naturally—they do so only when forced. Change requires energy. It is much more comfortable to exhibit little or no energy. That's why when we say, "Make yourself comfortable," a person sits down or reclines. They are seeking to exhibit less energy. So, when given the choice of keeping things as is and exhibiting the energy for change, people almost always opt for the former.

The problem is that the world is always changing. Our competitors don't wait on us to build up the energy to change. Somewhere, right now there is someone who is trying to figure out how to disrupt your business model. If you don't change it, the energy to change it will come from somewhere else.

Create systems in your business that force innovation. Make people regularly answer questions like, "What problems do our customers have that need to be solved?" or "If we started the business today, would we create this process the same way?" Take the answers to these questions and begin drilling down to understand the core reasons behind them. Once you truly understand a problem, potential solutions will start to become apparent. Demand that people in your business come up with ways to quickly test these solutions to see if any of them work, and if so, are they solving a big enough problem to warrant continuing on with the effort?

If you implement this kind of discipline in your business, you have to go into it knowing that most of the things you try will fail[4]. Failures are not merely steps we have to get past to succeed. Failures yield the

---

[4] I recommend the book *Rapid Results* by Robert H. Schaffer and Ronald N. Ashkenas for details on how to roll out this kind of discipline.

opportunities to learn that ultimately reveal solutions that succeed. The key to this is that you are purposeful not in trying to create successful innovations, but about learning from the many failures.

One of the goals of this principle is to fail in small, controlled environments where the risk is less than failing in big environments. Consider these alternatives:

In the first scenario, an executive hears a customer complain about a problem and has an idea for a new service that he thinks will be valuable to the company's customers in solving that problem. He spends weeks creating a plan and then goes to the upper brass to present the plan so that he can get the budget to roll it out. The presentation goes well, and he gets the budget. He hires some new people, moves others out of existing roles and onto this new team, spends months developing the technology to deliver the service, and then works with the marketing team on a big splash to alert all of the company's customers about the new service. After a million-dollar investment, a year of actual time, and several years of man-hours, the big debut goes out and...crickets. The customers aren't interested.

In the second scenario, an executive hears a customer complain about a problem and has an idea for a new service that he thinks will be valuable to the company's customers in solving that problem. Because he is expected to test something new every quarter, he mentions it to his team in their regularly scheduled innovation meeting. He asks them how they can most quickly determine if the proposed service will actually solve the customer's problem. They come up with some ideas that will allow them to produce a somewhat ugly but workable solution in 60 days that they could take to three customers. Because he already has some funds budgeted for exploring new ideas, he is able to immediately start on the proof-of-concept solution without having to wait on budget approval. So with just $10,000, 60 calendar days, and a month's worth of man-hours, they roll out the proof-of-concept and…crickets. The customers aren't interested.

So, which would you choose? The one that took a year to fail or the one that did so in 60 days?

But here is the rest of the story.

Both executives go to their customers and learn that with just a few tweaks, they will be able to provide something very valuable. In the second scenario, they do another quick project and deliver an adapted proof-of-concept product that the customers love. They roll out more customers on the ugly product while they go back and develop the much sleeker version. Meanwhile, the guy from the first scenario spends another year developing the new technology before he ultimately delivers the solution. Except his product is in the market 18 months after the other guy.

So, one guy spent 18 months doing the right thing, while the other guy was out in the market figuring out how to do it right.

Force everyone in your organization to innovate. Let them fail—at times, even when you could prevent it—and then reward the team that learns the most.

Fail-Safe vs. Excuse-Free

In Chapter 14, about the value of Growth, I mentioned that one of the phrases most often used by associates to describe our culture is "risk-free environment." "Fail-safe" is another one. I love that people know they can push the boundaries and try new things—that it is okay if they fail, as long as they learn from it.

But there is another side to this coin that people hardly ever mention: excuse-free. Our goal is that everyone has everything they need to succeed—including the ability to take chances. But if they fail, they are responsible. There are no excuses.

You could argue that this is an incredibly cruel thing to do to someone. But high-performance people love it. Give me the rope and I'll go scale that mountain. If I hang myself with it, then it was my own fault.

This sounds scary, but it's actually quite empowering. My job as a leader is to make sure you have everything you need to be successful—including permission to fail.

23
Use Smoke Alarms, Not Fire Alarms

I am fairly certain that there is a conspiracy among companies that make residential smoke alarms to deprive the American public of sleep. Why is it that the irritating beeping noise that smoke alarms emit to alert you that the batteries are low only goes off between one and four a.m.? Seriously, I can't remember ever hearing that noise in the middle of a Saturday afternoon. My memories of that noise always involve me in a bathrobe, standing bleary-eyed on a ladder, trying to figure out how in the world to disconnect the stupid thing from the ceiling mount.

However, there is one sound that is far worse than that of a smoke alarm in the middle of the night: the sound of a fire truck's siren rushing toward your house to put out a fire.

We'd all prefer to eliminate what's causing the smoke rather than try to salvage what remains after a fire. That is, preventing a problem, or detecting it early, is significantly less costly than fixing one after the fact.

We have all kinds of smoke alarms in the business—activity and production reports, sales funnels, associate surveys, customer surveys, reviews, skip-level meetings—the list goes on and on. These reports yield actionable data about how we are performing. They serve many purposes, but one of the main ones is to alert leaders as to when and where there might be a problem—while it is still solvable.

Every year we conduct a detailed survey of our associates to evaluate their satisfaction on a number of different issues. We look at each team and company and benchmark them against each other, prior years, and where we can, against other industry-leading companies. Fortunately for us, most teams consistently have very high scores.

One year I had a discussion with a leader who was advocating that we stop doing the surveys. The argument was that since the results were so positive every year, we weren't really learning anything new. Since we weren't seeing anything we should change or improve, we were wasting the time of all of our associates by asking them to take this exhaustive survey. It was an ineffective use of their time. (By the way, one rule we have is that people can't use my own arguments against me!)

I responded that as long as they were good results, we knew we didn't have any problems. But if we stopped asking the questions, how would we know that all remained well? What's more, the one time there is a problem is when we need these reports most. Without measuring associate satisfaction, we would only find out we have a problem when people start quitting. You may drive years without seeing the check engine light in your car, but when it does come on, you'd better pay attention, or you are about to have a much bigger problem.

Now there are certainly other ways of measuring associate satisfaction than a survey. The point is not that you should do an online survey versus in-person interviews or some other method. In a small business, you are probably so ingrained in the team that you can immediately tell when there is a problem. But once you reach any kind of scale, you have to put mechanisms in place to detect problems that people will otherwise hide.

I purposely use associate satisfaction as an example here. We are more naturally inclined to put in these smoke alarm type reports regarding production or operations. We watch these metrics, and when there is a problem, we swoop in to figure out what is going on. But we often take for granted the happiness of other people. Either through self-absorption or lack of caring, we fail to think about, much less inquire about, how associates feel about how things are going.

When it comes to individual satisfaction, it is particularly important that we ask the question. For many years, we have conducted individual annual reviews. This has gone out of vogue lately. The argument against annual reviews mainly rests on the theory that one shouldn't wait a year to give feedback. There should be an ongoing discussion about performance between a manager, employee, and team. I agree with this theory. However, it's human nature to get sucked into the "tornado" and forget to pull ourselves out to work on relationships with our people. Annual reviews require you to exert the energy it takes to ask questions about how people feel, really listen to them, give thoughtful feedback, and then adjust behavior. It is incredibly powerful for someone to feel like they have really been heard by someone in authority. I just don't trust myself (or others) to regularly have that conversation without the discipline of a process. Whether this process is monthly in a one-on-one, annually in a review, or in a survey (hopefully it is all of the above), it should be a regular thing.

Review your business for the things that could go wrong, and then set up smoke alarms to give you advanced warning when those things might happen. But make sure that the alarms include ways to get insights into how people on your team feel. If you don't make time to meet with them now, you will have to make the time later—when they tell you they are quitting.

24
You Don't Go Broke by Making Money

A couple of years ago, our family went on a long road trip out to the western part of the United States to see several of the amazing national parks. As we made our way back east through South Dakota, we took a detour of a couple hundred miles to a little town called De Smet, home of the Ingalls family homestead of Little House on the Prairie fame. My daughter (one of the few people I know who likes to read more than me) was eight years old at the time and had read all of Laura Ingalls Wilder's books. She was beside herself with excitement to see where Laura and her family actually lived.

One of the exhibits at the homestead was an example of a "dugout" frontier home. Pioneers who settled this prairie land typically arrived with some tools and only a little money. Most of them came from the East where forests grew plenty of wood for building homes, but out on the prairie, timber was hard to come by. So, needing to create shelter for their families, they would form a hut out of mud and sod by digging out the side of a hill. Like many other prairie pioneers, the Ingalls family lived in their dugout for a few years while they farmed and built up enough capital to afford lumber and other supplies needed for building a wood house.

The dugout was just one example of the ingenuity of these incredible people. When resources are few and survival is at stake, a person gets highly creative. A visitor might have sneered at the crudity of the way the pioneers lived and farmed, but they were able to survive in the most challenging of conditions. Those who survived the early, difficult years learned what it took to be successful and later used those lessons to thrive in the tough environment.

Entrepreneurs are the modern-day version of pioneers. I love hearing the stories entrepreneurs tell about the "early days" of their companies. They didn't have any money, so they had to get really creative to solve problems. When you can't afford to pay someone else to do something, you just figure out how to do it yourself. The entrepreneur is the salesperson, bookkeeper, IT department, and receptionist. He learns everything there is to know about what it takes to survive as a business. She intricately knows what her customers need and how to deliver it, because she had to figure out how to do it all.

Angel investors, venture capital, and private equity has changed the perception of what it means to be an entrepreneur. It used to be that the person with an idea would scrape and save every dollar to be able to launch a business and follow their passion. Today, that person often expects someone to write them a big check so they can hire a bunch of people to fill up their leased loft space with trendy furniture and a foosball table. They spend frivolously on marketing, price at a loss, and entertain customers lavishly. When the money runs out and they still don't have a profitable business model, they blame their investors' inability to see the big picture.

Okay, that's a bit of a stereotype, but unfortunately, it's not far from reality for many of today's startup companies.

I think our company has an advantage in our grass roots origins. A few people started our original businesses with limited amounts of capital. They had to figure out how to get profitable quickly, or they would be out of business. While we are now able to afford nice office spaces and entertainment for our associates and their families, we retain the entrepreneurial philosophy of figuring out creative solutions under the assumption of a necessity to quickly become profitable.

One of my dad's sayings is, "You don't go broke by making money." The message is that if you can figure out a profitable business model, you know you will continue to be in business. If your business makes money, you'll have the chance to chase the big opportunities. But if you aren't profitable, no such assurances exist.

Now of course we all know that "it takes money to make money," and sometimes you have to make big investments to solve big problems and get big returns. But the downside of this is that having money to throw at problems makes us sloppy. Wealth makes us lazy. When I can afford the downside, I don't learn from my mistakes because the ramifications of those mistakes are hidden.

When you are faced with a decision, it is often helpful to ask the question, "What would I do if I didn't have money to spend on the problem?" Even if you do have the money to spend, often the answer you come up with is the better answer. After all, if necessity is the mother of invention, what do you think happens when you don't need anything?

Someone's Livelihood Should Depend On It

Perhaps you have heard this classic business fable:

A pig and a chicken are walking down the road.

The chicken says to the pig, "Hey pig, I was thinking we should get involved in starting a restaurant together."

The pig replies, "What would we serve?"

To which the chicken answers, "Ham and eggs."

"No," the pig says. "You may be involved, but I would be committed."

While it helps, you don't have to be the business owner to be committed to the success of a business or project. Another saying I picked up from my dad is, "If something is important, then someone's livelihood should depend on its success."

The vice chairman of our company has an unorthodox way of creating organizational charts. He says to start by listing the critical success factors of the business—all the things it must do well to be successful. Then write a person's name next to each factor. Voilà, you have created your org chart and job descriptions at the same time.

Owners act differently than renters. Think about the way you treated the first home you owned versus the last apartment you rented. Owners take on a pride of ownership and show a responsibility that is apparent in the quality of their asset.

People on your team may not own the whole business, but they can still own some part of it. Let them be an owner and reap the benefits of the quality they create.

25
Distribute Information
(and Decentralize Decision Making)

Do you ever look back at your younger self and think what a fool you were? No? Am I the only one who does that?

In one of the first businesses I ran, I remember one time my head of sales (also known as my one sales guy) came to me asking when we were going to have all-hands team meetings. At that time, our company consisted of three people including me: one person to sell the deals, one person to support our few existing customers, and me who did everything else. We were hoping to make a sale that would enable us to hire employee number four soon.

I asked him, "Why do we need to meet with all three of us?"

"So that we all know everything that is going on," he answered.

I retorted, "I know everything that is going on. I'll meet with her and then with you, and I'll tell you what you need to know. You just focus on sales. There is no reason to waste your time on customer support issues."

In a last-gasp effort to convince me, he said, "I really think that the more I know about what our customers are experiencing with our product, the better I will be able to sell it."

I hate when other people are right.

Several years ago, Patrick Lencioni wrote a book called *Death by Meeting*. Like most of Lencioni's work, this is a well-written book with several valuable takeaways. However, this book caused a lot of problems—mostly among people who never actually read it. "Death by meetings" became a mantra among anyone who has ever gotten bored in a meeting. Suddenly they had a pop culture slogan to decry the old guard who liked to sit around and talk all the time versus actually getting things done. As a result, the anti-meeting crowd often threw out the good with the bad and swung organizations to the extreme where no one communicated.

A few years later, in a different business, I had a team member who complained about all the meetings she had to sit in. So I asked her which meetings she felt were a waste of her time (all of them), and I took her out of those meetings. Within a few months, she was back in my office complaining about how she didn't know what was going on in the business.

Hmmmm.

I was lamenting this dilemma to my dad one time, and he shared some words of wisdom: "It's not a question of whether being in a meeting is a good use of an individual's time; it's a question of whether it is a good use of the company's time."

Someone may be in a meeting where 75% of the agenda isn't applicable to them, but if even a few agenda items are necessary for them to do their job, should they be in that meeting? To answer the question, consider what organizational effort would be required to backtrack with that associate on the relevant items. The individual may have wasted 45 minutes of a one-hour meeting, but if it takes a combined three man-hours to circle back on the items they missed, which is the bigger waste?

We try to be very purposeful about meetings and who is in them. Like some of the suggestions Lencioni has in his book, we utilize agendas, minutes, action items, and parking lots. Every meeting has a stated purpose and is part of a bigger communication rhythm.

But this section is not about meetings. It is about the timely distribution of information (which sometimes takes place at meetings).

My goal is for everyone in our company to have all the information they need at the time they need it. Someone helping a customer needs to know everything necessary to solve the customer's problem right in that instant. If they have to go back to a manager to ask a question or call another department to get information, they lose an opportunity with that customer that we may never get back.

It's not enough to distribute information if people can't use it. Empower people to make decisions. The closer a person is to a customer, the better positioned they are to quickly service that customer. If they have to wait to get an approval from up the chain of command, then it will often be too late.

Many years ago, we purchased a company out of a distressed situation where the owner was engaging in nefarious dealings and misappropriating company funds. None of the managers had access to any financials (which were all fake anyway) because the owners had been trying to hide what they were doing. As a result, the managers had no idea what was making money for the business and what wasn't.

Shortly after we bought the company, the leadership received their first set of accurate financials in years. Before we even saw the numbers, they had already analyzed them and made a number of changes to their business—closing down some service lines and reallocating resources to areas where they could be better used.

Empowered, informed people will make decisions faster than you can as a manager and see things you will never see. Purposefully consider what information could be helpful to people and then utilize your reports, meetings, and all other communication to make sure they have that information as quickly as possible. But don't forget to give them the big picture. It is one thing to understand my little corner of the world, but when I understand how my corner fits into the world at large, I gain a context that may change how I approach things. I don't need to understand every detail about other parts of the company, but if I understand how what I do affects those downstream, I can be smarter about how I do what I do. Let me give you an example.

In our staffing businesses, we typically have salespeople who deal with our clients, and recruiters who interact with the doctors, nurses, or other professionals we staff. The personality of a salesperson is different from that of a recruiter, and it is pretty rare for someone to be good at (or enjoy) both jobs.

One time we had a successful recruiter, burned out with the 24/7 nature of the job, request to move into a sales role. These kinds of moves rarely succeed, but this was a hard worker who had been with us for several years. So with a warning about the risks involved, we let her make the move.

She was an instant success in sales.

Since this transition is rarely successful, we sought to understand why she had succeeded. It turned out she wasn't bringing in high volumes of new sales orders, which made it even more curious. What we discovered was that her recruiters had very high fill rates on the orders she had secured.

When asked, she explained: "Well, since I was a recruiter, I know what kind of orders they can fill. So as a salesperson, I only bring in those kinds of orders."

Continually provide people the information they need to do their jobs, make sure they know how they fit into the big picture, give them the authority to act, and then get out of their way.

Managerial Beliefs

Although the words occasionally get used interchangeably, there is a difference between leadership and management. Not all managers are leaders, but at some point, most leaders have to manage others. It is a skill set worth developing. Businesses need great leaders, but they also need great managers. What follows are a few of our beliefs about management.

26
Associates are Volunteers; Managers are Stewards

At Jackson Healthcare, we purposely use the word "associate" and not "employee." Not that there is anything wrong with the word "employee"—it simply means a person who works for wages or salary. "Associate," on the other hand, means a partner or colleague.

Our use of the word "associate" stems from our acknowledgment of the value of each individual and our recognition that it takes a team to deliver services to our customers. We have no class system—no person is more important than another, and all of us work together as partners.

It also reminds us as managers that the people on our teams are here voluntarily. They entered into an agreement to perform certain work in exchange for payment in the form of wages. It is a mutually agreed upon exchange. Each person can and should be held accountable for performing work to their best ability and consistent with the agreed-upon quality.

However, indentured servitude ended many years ago. Just because someone reports to you on an organizational chart does not mean that you are the master of their life. It does not mean that they must endure your cruelty with no other option. If they don't like the way you treat them, guess what they are free to do?

Leave.

They are volunteers not in the sense that they work for free, but in the sense that they are there of their own volition. Out of their own free will, they have placed themselves under your direction as a manager.

So what does that mean? What impact can you as a manager have on the life of someone you are managing?

A huge impact, as it turns out.

As a manager you arguably have a bigger, more direct impact on the well-being of the people who report to you than any other person in their life. At a minimum, you impact their ability to generate income. If you approve of their work, they could get a raise and make more money. You may control whether or not they get a bonus. If you disapprove of their work, not only might they make less money, but you have the ability to terminate their employment, thus placing a black mark on their résumé that may prevent them from making as much money in the future or gaining future employment at all.

But it's more than just money. Managers have a huge impact on the self-esteem of the people who work for them. As a key judge of their performance, your approval can lift spirits, while your disapproval can cause a person to question their own worth. You can increase stress or relieve it. By setting a schedule, you influence the amount of time an individual has to spend with their family, exercise, or explore personal interests.

You influence a person's growth. You can provide access to education and experiences that make them capable of increased contribution and greater marketability. You can push them, or you can hold them back from opportunities that will challenge them. You can shine a light on their efforts or make sure they never get credit for what they do.

Your decisions as a manager will impact people's marriages, friendships, families, careers, and even their health. That is a powerful influence.

The people you manage have given you this power over them. You didn't take it or force it, they willingly gave it to you. They have put great trust in you to wield the power wisely. They expect you to use it for their best interest. They have agreed to take your direction in guiding their daily activities, and in exchange, they expect you to help them achieve things in their lives that they cannot achieve on their own.

So what will you do with this role of manager? How will you approach the people over whom you exert this influence? How will you handle this great responsibility?

The concept of stewardship first appeared in the Middle Ages. It denoted a person who was the manager of a large household. A steward was the person who cared for the owner's home in his stead. He was given the responsibility for overseeing something that he did not own. Since that time, the concept of stewardship has grown. Merriam-Webster defines stewardship as "the careful and responsible management of something entrusted to one's care."

Your employees, associates, team members—however you refer to the people you manage or oversee—they have entrusted something very precious to your care. You are indeed a steward over a big part of their lives, and that demands careful and responsible management.

As I stated earlier, corporate culture can often be boiled down to how your boss treats you. Certainly, the main reason people quit jobs is because of a misalignment of values and beliefs, but the primary source of this misalignment is usually with their direct manager. Far more people quit managers than quit companies. If your manager doesn't treat you with respect, look out for your best interest, or help you achieve more than you could on your own, how long would you work for them?

Being a manager is a special calling. It is not just a way to make more money or climb the corporate ladder. It is a great honor when someone chooses to work under your direction. Your stewardship of this honor deserves the seriousness, purposefulness, and dedication befitting this tremendous responsibility.

When to Let Them Fail

Unfortunately, there are some lessons that are difficult to learn until you experience them. I once heard someone say, "Good judgment comes from wisdom; wisdom comes from bad judgment." Sometimes you have to make the mistake and suffer the consequences of a bad decision to be able to truly understand how to do it better in the future.

Parents think about this often when their kids are young. It is a necessary part of learning to walk that a child falls down a few times. There's just no other way to learn. I remember when I taught my kids to ride a bike, I knew going into the lessons that there were going to be some scraped knees and tears as part of the process. So I had the antiseptic and Band-Aids at the ready as we headed outside. Unfortunately, no one learns to ride a bike without a couple of tumbles.

A big part of a parent's job is to create an atmosphere where a child can make the mistakes necessary to learn such that the ramifications of these mistakes are acceptable. We want them to learn the lessons when the stakes are low versus when they are high.

In our school system, transitioning from elementary to middle school involves big changes. Instead of sitting in one room all day, the kids go from room to room for each class. They have to learn to get the right books and materials to the class in the short period of time between each session. The teachers no longer give them as many reminders of when assignments are due, and so they have to keep track of homework and projects to make sure they are turned in on time. When our son made this transition, my wife worked with him at the beginning of the school year to come up with his system of organization, but it soon became apparent that he had transferred his organizational dependence from his teacher to his mom. So after a few weeks, she stopped helping and made him fully responsible. We both knew that the transition wouldn't go smoothly. Sure enough, a few weeks later when the report cards came, we saw that he had a lower than usual grade in one of his best subjects. Turns out that he had aced the tests but had forgotten to turn in a couple of homework assignments, which had brought down his grade in the class. He was upset, but it led to him really owning his organizational system for school. Our view was that it is better for him to learn the lesson in sixth grade than when he gets to college.

I hate using parenting analogies when talking about managers, because it can come across as condescending—as if we view the people we manage as children. This is certainly not the case, but there are many parallels between the two. As we discussed in this chapter, managers are stewards over a great part of the lives of their associates. We must decide when to let someone do something that we know will be a mistake so that they can learn a lesson only experience will teach. A big part of that judgment is ensuring the ramifications of the mistake won't be unacceptable for the associate or the company.

27
Hire for Culture

Is there anything harder than trying to determine if someone is going to be successful in a given job? Whole industries have been spawned to try and help companies figure out how to hire the right people. There are countless books, seminars, tests, and techniques created by consultants and self-anointed experts claiming to have the solution to this daunting task.

I do not claim to be such an expert.

But entrepreneurs are smart to tap into this market. They are targeting a huge potential customer base (virtually every company that exists) with a significant problem. Their customers understand the upside of hiring the right person and the big downside of hiring the wrong person.

We know that the main reason people quit or get fired from a job is because of a misalignment between their values and beliefs and those of the company, team, or (most often) manager. Certainly, there are many terminations based on competency (someone just doesn't have the skills to do the job), but if you have any kind of interview process at all, chances are that you have become at least somewhat adept at determining skills. In our organization, termination based on someone not having the skills necessary to do a job happens far less frequently than those due to issues of values and beliefs. This is why, as I discussed in Chapter 9, a primary objective of the interview process must be to reveal the candidate's values and beliefs.

The challenge is that most interviewing techniques and skills have been created to reveal competency. A résumé tells you what a person has done, not why they did it. Most of the questions we ask are crafted to pull out what an individual is good or bad at based on their experience or knowledge about certain things. We have exhaustive skills or knowledge tests, especially for developers, accountants, and other hard skill positions. I would even include most personality testing in the bucket of competency. They are designed to determine if a candidate's personality shows a fitness for a specific type of job.

All of these things are very important and by no means should be abandoned. But competency should be table stakes. If you don't have the skills, knowledge, or personality to do the job, then you don't even get a chance.

How well they will fit in with the culture of the team is what should ultimately determine which of the competent candidates gets the job.

Sound pretty straightforward? Well, it's rather hard. Mostly it's hard because we have so little experience doing it—at least in a business setting.

So, let's go outside of business to something much easier—marriage (said with tongue firmly planted in cheek). If you are married, think a minute about the process you went through in choosing a spouse. If you aren't married, think about how you came to be close with a good friend. Some people date for years, and some people fall in love at first sight and pop the question on the first date (at least that's what happens in the movies), but most of us go through some version of the same process.

We meet and there is an initial attraction. The attraction is caused either consciously or subconsciously because the other person fits a description of someone that could fill some physical and emotional needs for you. (Yeah, I know this sounds really romantic!) Assuming the other person is attracted to you as well, you start spending more time together. During this courting process, you explore deeper to see if your initial impression was correct. You do this through long talks and going through many experiences together. You see how the person acts and reacts in certain situations. You introduce the person to friends and family who know you well in order to get their opinions as to whether this will be a good fit. You are trying to figure out if they value the things you value and believe the things you believe. Do you have enough commonality on important matters such that you could make a lifelong commitment together?

Think about the time and effort you put into dating and choosing a spouse. Now I am not saying that hiring is dating, nor am I saying that hiring a person you work with is as important as choosing a spouse. But the processes aren't so different—or at least, they shouldn't be.

Most interviews don't get us beyond the initial attraction phase. This person seems to fit the overall definition of who I'm looking for, so I hire them. The problem is that instead of dating, we go right to getting married.

Build the dating phase into your hiring. Try to determine candidates' closely held values and beliefs through seeing how they act and react to given situations. Ask people who know you well to tell you whether or not they think the candidate will be a good fit.

But enough theory. Here are some real suggestions for interviewing:

- Ask behavioral questions that focus on relationships with other people. Get descriptions of people and situations where they worked well or didn't and why. What attracted them to a certain job? Why did they leave? What was different about that job from what they expected? When did they feel successful? Out of place? Ask about people they got along with and didn't. If they have been a manager, delve into people who worked well for them and those who quit or had to be terminated. What drove those terminations? And of course, ask why, why, why. The underlying issues in these situations give you clues about what they value.

- Conduct lots of interviews with lots of people. One time I met with someone in talent acquisition at a very successful, well-known company and asked how they determined fit. He told me that each candidate has to go through 15 interviews, and each interviewer is asked to determine if that person will fit in with the team. "If they can get the thumbs up from 15 people," he said, "they're either a really good actor or they'll fit in just fine."

- Going back to the dating analogy, if all of your friends and family tell you they think your new girlfriend is a perfect fit for you, it offers reassurance about your prospects with her. On the contrary, if everyone you love and trust tells you that it will never work, my guess is that would at least give you pause. Ask as many people as you can justify to interview a serious candidate. It can make for a long process for the candidate, so you will want to coordinate the interviewers such that they are asking different questions and not being needlessly repetitive. Afterwards, ask each interviewer if they think the candidate will fit in, and pay a lot of attention to their answers.

- Be blunt. When all else fails, don't be afraid to ask questions that really put candidates on the spot. For example, "Our people regularly take short-term hits on their commission when they need to resolve a problem for a customer. Tell me about a time when you made a short-term sacrifice for a long-term goal." It's not only important as to whether they actually have an example of delayed gratification, but also look at the reaction to the question. Is the premise of the question shocking, or do they seem comfortable?

Keep in mind that the goal is not just for you to screen out candidates who won't fit in; ideally you also want candidates to screen themselves out. The sooner someone comes to a realization that the values and beliefs of your business don't line up with theirs, the sooner they will opt out, saving you and your team from wasting any more time with them. It's hard to screen for values, and many people will fool you. So if you can get them to screen themselves out, it will make your job as the interviewer much easier.

If neither of you realize that there is a value misalignment until after they start, they will quit and you will have wasted everyone's time and effort. The more transparent you are about your values and beliefs in the interview process (and even in the content you provide before the interview), the more likely a mismatched candidate will be to take themselves out of the process before you do.

28
Hires Refine Your Culture; Fires Define It

It is entertaining to listen to pundits analyze sports teams at the end of a season. They analyze strengths and weaknesses of players and pontificate about which positions a team needs to improve. Every year you hear about the team who is just "one player away" from becoming championship caliber. If they can just upgrade skills at one guard position or one wide receiver, then that will make the difference.

And sometimes it does. It is amazing what a difference one person can make on the team. Their positivity changes the attitude of the team. Their work ethic sets an example that makes everyone else work harder. They bring that missing element that makes everyone else better.

But of course, the opposite can also be true. Nothing will kill a team faster than a talented player with a negative attitude.

Businesses are no different. Each hire makes a team perform better or worse. There is no neutral. Some hires move the needle significantly and others only slightly, but every person impacts the team.

As we just discussed, if you are hiring for cultural fit, you have the opportunity to reinforce or refine your culture. But nothing says you mean what you say about values more than firing someone over a values issue.

One of the ongoing disagreements I have with Human Resources professionals is around what is communicated when someone is terminated. The typical approach that HR advocates is to be as generic as possible about what is said publicly regarding why someone is let go, so as to not say anything that could give rise to a wrongful termination suit.

Hogwash. If someone is fired—especially over a blatant disagreement over our values or core beliefs—I want everyone to know why.

And the higher profile the better.

Several years ago, I made a decision to hire a senior executive for our team. We infrequently hire senior executives from the outside, and there was a lot of attention on this hire. This person came from a Fortune 50 business and had an impressive résumé. We "paid up" to get him, going above our budget to win top talent for this key position, and we spent a lot of money to move him to Atlanta.

Less than 60 days into his tenure, someone came to me saying that they had seen a young lady on his team crying. After asking what had happened, they learned that this new executive had berated her in front of the team when she questioned something he had asked them to do. Upon investigation, I learned that it was actually worse, as he had told her that he was a vice president, she was just a "worker bee," and that she needed to learn that her place was to do what she was told and not question a vice president.

I fired him that very afternoon.[5]

---

[5] This was before I established some of my current philosophies on interviewing and was actually a key experience in forming some of them. In fact, several of the people on my team who interviewed him had indeed told me that they didn't think he would fit in, and I ignored their feedback.

But here is the powerful part. I called his entire team into a conference room to say the following:

"You all know that John was a big hire for us. It took us several months to find him, and we paid a lot of money to move him here. We did it because this is an important team that plays a critical role in our company.

"However, there is no one in this company who is more important, more valuable, or whose opinion matters more than anyone else. I heard what happened in your meeting this morning with Sally. If that happened today, I'm sure there are several other instances of disrespect that I don't know about (turns out there were). No one gets to work here if they don't show respect to other people. This is why I fired John today.

"My job is to provide you with everything you need to be successful—and that includes providing you with the right leader. I failed in doing that for you. But I will learn from this and figure out how to do a better job next time."

There were tears in the room—certainly not because they were sad to see John leave—but they were moved that I would terminate a high-profile, newly-hired senior executive in a strategic position because he showed disrespect to a person who was literally on the bottom of the organization chart. Each person on the team is that important.

No one is above our values. Not even a vice president or the highest producing salesperson.

Now that brings up a tough question. What do you do when you have someone who is bringing in a ton of business and making a lot of money for the company, but treats people terribly? This is where the rubber meets the road—when you have to show what you truly value. How do you handle someone who is clearly behaving outside the values and beliefs of the company, but generating a lot of profit?

I wish I could say that I have always made the choice to enforce values and fired people when they blatantly operated against our values. Admittedly, there have been times where I let the fear of losing that person and their ability to generate revenue get in the way of what I knew was the right thing to do. I will tell you now that I have regretted every time I succumbed to that fear. Every time I let someone hang around who behaved in opposition to our values there was collateral damage that more than offset the financial gain. And every time, I felt that I lost credibility with my team. Each time they heard me talk about our values, but not correct or dismiss someone who opposed them, it undermined my message and the team's confidence in me.

A few years ago, after playing out this scenario one too many times, I consciously released the fear of losing a top performer and made the decision never to fall for it again.

There is **no such thing** as a **star performer who is a cancer.**

One time a leader asked me what to do with a star performer who is a cancer on the team.

"There is no such thing," I told them. "You can't be a cancer and a star performer."

It is easier for someone in my position, leading a company as profitable as ours, to say you should terminate someone over values issues. I can afford that loss, but this is not always the case for others in our company. There have been many times where a manager or business leader who worked with me was in a situation where letting someone go was going to cost them and their business dearly. The impact might have been minimal for me, but it was not to them. However, in all these situations and despite the cost, I have never had someone come back to me and say that they regretted cutting out the cancer.

I am not saying that we should be quick to fire people in all situations. The preference is always to coach them to see the error of their ways, and hopefully they learn that there is a better way of doing things. Often just the fear of losing their job is enough to get them to change their behavior, but nothing causes that fear as much as seeing someone else get fired for that very reason.

As a leader, people are hyper-tuned to what you say and what you do. As a manager, they are specifically paying attention to what you say versus what you allow other people to do. Over the long term, you will always be glad you stood up for your values. Despite the short-term cost, the gain will be great.

29
Situational Leadership

If there was only one management theory I would suggest you learn, it is situational leadership. I can claim no authorship whatsoever of this theory, but I wholeheartedly endorse it. I'll summarize it here, but to really understand the theory of situational leadership, consider reading *Leadership and the One Minute Manager: Increasing Effectiveness Through Situational Leadership* by Ken Blanchard or *The Situational Leader* by Dr. Paul Hersey.

The net of the theory (in my words) is this: your management style should reflect the needs of the person you are managing, not the style you prefer. Based upon a person's experience with and mastery of tasks associated with a role (their readiness), a manager must adjust how he directs and communicates.

Micromanagement has a terrible reputation. I have asked dozens of people across the years to describe their management style, and 90% or more have begun their answer by saying, "Well, I'm not a micromanager." Consider this: if you are brand new to a role or have no idea how to accomplish an assigned task, what do you want from your manager? More than likely you would want very clear, specific instructions with frequent inspection and feedback on every detail. But isn't that the very definition of micromanaging? On the contrary, what if your manager gave you a project about which you had no knowledge or experience and said, "I don't want to micromanage you, so

I'm just going to leave you alone. Good luck figuring it out!" That would be setting you up for failure, and frankly, a cruel act by a manager.

Micromanaging is not intrinsically bad, though it gets a bad rap because it is often used inappropriately—in the wrong circumstances and at the wrong time.

People go through varying stages of competency at their job. At first, they need lots of direction. At other times, they know how to do the job, but still need encouragement. Ultimately, most people reach a point where they are experts. They require neither a manager's direction nor encouragement. They only need their manager occasionally to clear roadblocks and provide accountability.

Perhaps what is so attractive to me about the situational leadership theory is that it epitomizes our value, Others First. The point is to think about what the other person needs, not what you as a manager need.

One time I worked with a manager who had turned over his entire team during the course of a year. Literally every person on the team had been replaced. They had all either quit or been fired for an inability to perform and hit goals. I asked the manager what he thought had happened.

"The problem," he said, "is that we had a lot of inexperienced people. My management style is that we agree on the objective, and then I trust people to do their jobs. I am used to working with professionals. These people just couldn't cut it on their own."

We reviewed the experience of the people on the team. Some of them were young and inexperienced, but some had plenty of industry experience. However, they were all new to the role and to the company.

"The problem," I told him, "is that you think managing is about you. It's not. It's about them. Stop focusing on how you like to manage and start managing the way your people need you to."

One of the keys to situational leadership is what the authors call negotiating. This is simply a discussion between the manager and the associate regarding the level of readiness the associate has for various parts of her job. Subsequently, the two then agree on the management style that the manager should use for that part of the job. When both parties know and agree upfront on management style, there are no hard feelings about being over- or under-managed—as long as this is an ongoing discussion.

I make sure to regularly ask the people I work with if we are meeting too frequently or infrequently or if they feel like they need more or less direction from me in certain areas. These are empowering conversations as it gives the associate a voice (and subsequently, buy-in) in the way they are being managed.

Situational leadership is really just the value, Others First, applied to a manager/associate relationship. And just like in other situations, considering the needs of others is often the best way to get what you need. Even as a manager.

New Manager and New People

Here is another one of my dad's maxims: never have new managers manage new people. The problem is that neither one knows what they are doing. If you consider the situational leadership model, people who are new to a position need lots of direction including detailed instruction, frequent inspection, and feedback. A manager who is new to the role is unqualified to do this. It's the managerial equivalent of the blind leading the blind and is fraught with peril.

However, often good managers are placed in charge of teams about which the manager knows very little. A new manager doesn't have to know on the first day the details of how the team or employee performs its duties if she is leading experienced people. In fact, it can be quite advantageous and is an opportunity to use situational leadership somewhat in reverse. When someone is new to their role, they need lots of communication to learn. Similarly, communication needs to be frequent as the manager learns from her employees about the jobs they do.

It is vital that the manager communicate the purpose of this frequent communication up front, or else it may be interpreted negatively by the team. Imagine if you had been in a job for several years and were considered an expert at what you do. Suddenly you have a new manager and they are talking to you all the time about how you do your job. How dare they? They are brand new, and they have the audacity to come in here and question how I do my job?

In contrast, if handled correctly, this can be empowering for the associate and a great start to the new manager relationship. Plus, it provides an opportunity for a new manager to ask questions out of what we call "intelligent ignorance." Because they don't know anything about how things are done, they can ask about why things are done a certain way. Many times, the answer is "because they've always been done that way." This typically means the task could be done better or may not need to be done at all.

Whether it's a new team member or a new manager, someone with a fresh perspective is likely to discover opportunities for improvement—just as long as both of them aren't new.

30
Align Incentives

I was exasperated. And my management team could not understand what was happening.

"These people just don't see the big picture," someone said. "They need to think about the needs of the company and not just themselves."

Sorry, let me back up.

It is not uncommon for us to have different entities within Jackson Healthcare that either directly or indirectly compete with each other. Sometimes they provide the exact same service (our two largest companies both provide temporary staffing of physicians) and sometimes they provide different services that can solve the same problem (temporarily providing a CFO versus placing someone full-time).

The people in our company overwhelmingly get along. They are a part of a Jackson Healthcare company because they love the mission of improving the lives of others. They go out of their way to help each other, even if there isn't anything in it directly for them.

But sometimes they compete. They do so respectfully (for the most part), but they are still competing.

From time to time, someone (typically in corporate management) has an idea that two of these competing teams could work together in some way to help the company as a whole. This sounds great in theory, but it never works.

It was after one of these failed, grand "synergy" projects that my team was so frustrated. "How can they not see that what we were asking was for the greater good?"

Finally, I shut everyone up. "The problem," I said, "is that we are providing incentives for them to do one thing and asking them to do something else."

No one on those teams got a commission check for the greater good. People didn't get bonuses if another JH company hit its budget but the team they lead didn't. And promotions weren't going to be handed out to people who failed to hit their own goals—even if they had helped others to hit theirs.

Now maybe those bonus plans should be restructured, but that is not the point here. The point is that what we reward is what gets done. Be it compensation, recognition, or advancement, whatever gets people the reward they desire is what they will do.

Therefore, it is vitally important to reward the right things. Our goal for incentives is this—when the associate wins, the company wins. Whatever it is that causes an associate to earn a commission or receive a bonus means they did something that caused the company to hit its goals.

My dad tells about an epiphany he had many years ago when he realized that he was the only one who cared about the bottom line. Everyone else in the company was paid based on revenue. Well, he decided that he no longer wanted to be the only person who was losing sleep about whether or not the company was profitable, so he made everyone's bonus based on the bottom line. Suddenly, there were a lot more people thinking about expenses.

Lots of other people losing sleep over profits meant that he no longer had to lose sleep.

A few years ago, we bought a company whose leaders were all paid on revenue. Shortly after we bought them, they began losing money. Business volume had gone down, and yet they still had the same size back office staff. No one likes layoffs, but clearly, we had too many people for what the business needed. I asked the leaders to come up with a plan to reduce staff. They came back and said that everyone was busy and that we couldn't afford to let anyone go, or we would suffer a reduction in quality that would put all our customer relationships at risk. Not too much later I changed their bonus plans so that they were paid on the bottom line instead of revenue. They were aghast.

"You can't do this to us! It's not fair!"

"Why not?"

"The business is so overstaffed we can't possibly be profitable. You have to get rid of the extra people before we can go on a profit-based compensation plan."

You can't make this stuff up.

I know that people will figure out how to work whatever plan you give them. If there is a loophole, they will find it. And I'm okay with that if it means the company wins too. Be very careful to create incentives that reward behavior that is good for the company.

And don't be surprised when they act the way they have been incented to act.

Dual Reports

Years ago, I had a lady who reported both to me and to another part of the business. She rarely hit her goals, usually claiming that she was having to spend her time on the other manager's projects. After a few months of this, I finally went to the other manager to complain that she was asking too much of our joint report, and as a result, I wasn't getting any of my projects done. "Funny," she said. "She never gets anything done for me either because she says she is always doing things for you."

Turns out this was an individual whose primary skill was hiding in the chaos. That conversation shortly led to a termination, but her failure was not solely her fault. We put her in a position where priorities were not clearly defined. We didn't properly define success and align her incentives to those of the company.

And to this day, I don't like it when people have dual reports. If someone reports to two people, they don't report to anyone.

31
Manage Activities, Not Results

If you are able to endure enough pain, you can complete
a triathlon without training. Over the years, I have known a
few people who didn't like to train but enjoyed racing (or more
accurately, they enjoyed telling people that they were triathletes).
So a few weeks before a race, they would go for a couple swims
and runs, get on their bikes a time or two, and then head off for
the race. They weren't fast, but they could finish. And then they
would be in a world of hurt for a few days.

I had a friend like this who occasionally came out to race with
me. After one race, I asked him how he felt.

"Disappointed," he said.

"Why?"

"I finished with a worse time than last year. I was hoping to be
faster this year."

Really?

I could make a point here about hope not being a strategy, but
I'll save that for another time.

I often tell people that a triathlon is a lagging indicator of
fitness. You are fit (or not) before you do the triathlon. Racing
just confirms it. Racing doesn't make you faster; it confirms that
your training—the things that you did before the race—made
you faster.

One of the things I like to ask new managers is what metrics
they will focus on as they run their teams. The answer is almost

always EBITDA (probably because it is the basis of their bonus). "What else?" I ask. That's when I usually get blank stares. "What numbers can you look at to know whether or not you will hit EBITDA budget before financials come out?" More blank stares.

Everything that happens is a result of some activity that happened before. There is virtually nothing we can do to change today, but everything we do today will change tomorrow.

There is virtually **nothing** we can do to **change today,** but **everything we do today will change tomorrow.**

Just as the outcome of a triathlon is a result of your training, EBITDA is the result of specific activities that take place in your business—the question is which activities.

Search for the leading indicators—the activities that drive the results of your business. When I was running LocumTenens.com, I could look at one number each month and predict whether or not we were going to hit our budget. You should know what the most important metric is in your business—if you don't, then you don't understand what drives your business. I am not saying that there aren't multiple activities that drive the business and many metrics you should monitor, but usually there are a very small few that really tell the tale.

Once an executive asked if he could schedule a couple hours with me so I could show him which reports I looked at for the business. "I'm happy to show you," I said, "but it won't take two hours. About 15 minutes should do."

I'm not saying I only spend 15 minutes reviewing financial statements, but what I look at in detail will change each month. When I review a report, or even our financial statements, there are a few important numbers I always look at first, and then depending on what they are, I know where to dig in from there.

As a manager and the person who creates the priorities for your team, it is important that you know what the key activities are that drive your business. People get distracted by any number of tasks that may be interesting but have little to no impact on achieving their goals. It is your job as a leader to keep people focused on and performing the activities that will make them successful.

I'm often asked how I manage my time, and I typically respond by saying, "I'll be happy to tell you, but it may not help you all that much."

The reason is this: I am maniacally focused on only doing important things. As I plan my day or week—and constantly throughout every day—I ask myself the question, "Is this the most important thing I could be doing right now?"

The reason this insight isn't always helpful is because in order to apply it in your own life, you have to be able to recognize what is important based on your definition of success. As I discussed in Chapter 17, if you haven't taken the time to articulate where you want to go, it's impossible to know which activities are most likely to get you there.

Because I know my personal mission and my values, I am able to filter activities as either pushing me toward fulfilling that mission in a way that is consistent with my values or not. If not, then I don't do it. If yes, then I stack it up against the other activities that are on mission and make a judgment as to which will have the biggest impact.

The problem with this time management strategy is that it means you often say "no." And that makes you rather unpopular with the people on the other end of that "no." I have simply made the decision that I would rather be unpopular with a few people if it means making a bigger impact with my life.

I wish I could say that I live out this theory perfectly. Of course I don't. I struggle with spending my time on things that are inconsistent with my professed values like we all do. But lots of practice helps. And once you start saying no to people, you get better at it.

Whether you are managing a team or yourself, you need to know the activities that are effective at driving you toward success. Focus on those things. Develop metrics around these leading indicators and hold yourself and your team accountable.

Focus on the right activities, and the results will come.

32
Replace Yourself

One of the jobs of any leader is to make themselves dispensable. Leaders do this by coaching and developing people to do what they do.

Several years ago, I was speaking to a group of managers about this concept of training your replacement. I could feel the discomfort in the room. People were too quiet. Finally, some brave person spoke up and said, "But if we train our replacement, then you don't need us. Doesn't that create job insecurity for us?"

As an answer, I listed out the managers that we had in the company. "Now, help me figure out how many of these people at one time worked for or were mentored by Katie.[6]"

I don't remember the exact number, but it was around 40%. Almost half of the managers in our company had been trained by Katie and then moved to another team that needed a leader.

"I would tell all of you today," I said, "that Katie could leave and her team wouldn't miss a beat. Frankly, her team doesn't really need her to keep performing.

"So, what do you think? Should we fire Katie? She has a big salary, so it would really save the company money. Everyone on the profit-sharing plan would get a bigger bonus."

---

[6] That is her real name and she is one of the best I have ever known at coaching and developing other people.

Obviously, there was no way we would fire the person who had trained 40% of our managers and continued to churn out more leaders from under her tutelage.

There is also a corporate stewardship argument for replacing yourself as a leader. Part of your job is to make sure that the company is positioned to thrive after you have gone—building for legacy, as we say. Leaving your team unable to function when you leave is a dereliction of duty.

But there are also valid, purely selfish reasons for replacing yourself. In our company, you must replace yourself before you can be promoted. This is partly because it makes no sense to move someone from one team to another to solve a problem for the new team and create a problem for the old one. But it is also because we believe that as a leader, one of your primary jobs is to develop your people. If you have been unable to do this to the point that they can get along without you, then it means you haven't done a good enough job as a leader to deserve a promotion.

As a leader, one of your primary jobs is to **develop your people.**

People who become managers and stay managers do so because they enjoy contributing to the growth of other people. If you don't take pleasure in other people's successes, you will quit being a manager, because otherwise it's not worth all the hassles and frustrations. As a steward of the trust your employees have put in you, you owe it to them to focus on how to help them grow. But more than that, the satisfaction of seeing someone succeed and knowing you played a part in that success is incredible.

Being someone who can help others grow is not easy. It takes purposeful focus on actions that allow and sometimes force growth. It means letting people make mistakes so they can learn from them—even when you could have prevented the mistake. It involves setting aside the time to really listen and understand someone else's goals and desires. It means exerting the energy to direct and communicate with them the way they need, even when it would be quicker and easier to communicate the way you would prefer. Few people are actually willing, much less able, to really help the people they manage to grow.

But a leader who is able to make himself totally dispensable is himself totally indispensable.

Relational Beliefs

Regardless of your profession, relationship status, or where you live, one thing we have in common is that eventually, we are all going to have to deal with other people. In most business settings, to effectively do our jobs, we have to communicate and work with many different people all the time. In this section, I will discuss a few of our philosophies that impact how we communicate and work with others.

33
Environments Matter

One of the recurring discussions we have amongst the leaders of our company is about dress code—the old debate about what we should wear to the office. Business? Business casual? Casual? Pajamas? What qualifies as business casual? Can women wear leggings? What about casual Fridays? Are t-shirts allowed? Ugh.

Several years ago, in one of these discussions, someone was arguing that being required to wear a certain type of clothing to work was an outdated concept. "I can be just as productive wearing jeans as I can a suit," he pointed out. "In fact, I'd probably be more productive because a suit is so uncomfortable."

This is a valid point, but you cannot deny that wearing different types of clothing makes you feel differently and act differently. Regardless of how comfortable you are, when you wear a tuxedo or formal gown, you feel more, well, formal. And generally, you act more formally as well. You certainly act differently than when you are wearing gym clothes.

My adversary in this discussion was still not convinced. "That just means you are being fake. I'm the same person no matter what I wear."

I tried a different tack. "What would you think if you went to see a movie about the Civil War, and instead of wearing soldier uniforms, the actors all wore 1980's era sweat suits?"

"Well, that's different. That wouldn't fit their roles."

But don't we play different roles in our lives? We play our work role, our friend role, our parent role, or our sibling role. In each of these roles, we speak differently, act differently, even hold our posture differently.

If you played sports, you remember feeling the difference between the practice uniform and the game uniform. When you put the game uniform on, it just felt different. It hung a little heavier or fit a little better. But mainly, you remember how it made you feel—it's game time. Time for the adrenaline to get going.

As an actor, I have played many different roles. When you take on a new role, you attempt to get into the mindset of that character in that setting. You work to feel less like yourself and more like the character. It may not happen right away, but once you put on the costume and see yourself in the mirror, something changes. You truly feel different.

This isn't just about clothing. The set, the props, everything on stage or in a movie has to be right. It helps the actor, but more importantly, it communicates vital information to the audience. Every detail about what is seen and heard has to be right in order to effectively transport the viewer to that time and place.

I was not always in tune to the impact that environment can have on a person. When I first got married, I was moving out of my man cave house that I shared with other single buddies and into a home with a woman for the first time. At first, I was skeptical about all the decorating that she wanted to do—I mean that bean bag was perfectly comfortable. But since I wanted to stay married for a while, I decided to let her do her thing.

One day I entered a room she had recently decorated and turned to her and said, "I love coming into this room. I just love the way it makes me feel."

My wife is too big of a person to say "I told you so" and just took my changed attitude as a compliment.

Spaces affect how we feel, how we think, and how we relate. We have done everything we can (and some may say gone overboard) in creating an atmosphere in our offices that make people feel like they are somewhere special, and therefore, they should act special.

Recently I hired an executive who spent years working in another industry. She said, "I used to be so cheap when it came to spending money on the office environment. Who cares? It's just the place we work. If you want to be somewhere nice go to your house or a trendy restaurant. But I have totally changed that view since coming to work here. Every day I come in and am surrounded by beauty. It inspires me to act in a beautiful way. Plus, it makes me actually want to be in the office, so I guess that's good for the company!"

I am a fan of company meetings. I think they are times to not only update everyone in the company with the big picture and other information they need to do their job, but also to cast a vision and create a picture of where we are going and who we are. For years, I would drive the team that helped me put on these meetings crazy with all the details I insisted on directing and personally inspecting. I insisted on checking the lighting, video, and sound. I wanted a specific dress code for anyone who was going to be speaking. One time, someone said to me, "It's just a company meeting; this isn't the theater."

"Oh but isn't it?" I replied. "I'm trying to create the right atmosphere for people to learn and be inspired. If there are things in the environment that distract from that, then the message gets watered down and we will be wasting our time."

Over the years, that team learned my idiosyncrasies and took pride in creating the perfect environment for our meetings.

Creating an environment conducive to communication isn't just about offices or company meetings though. It's just as important in one-on-one settings.

I know a guy who once played offensive lineman on a football team at a Division I school. This is a huge guy. An injury kept him from going pro, but he still looks like he could easily go push around some defenders today. It cracks me up when I hear him speak to one of his young children. He crouches down to them, his voice goes up an octave, and his words sound more like cooing than English. Can you imagine this massive guy on the football field cooing at his teammates as they drive down the field?

Acting differently in different situations and with different people doesn't necessarily mean you are being fake. It means that you are communicating in the style and method that is most effective for the other person. You would never speak to your children using the same tone or language you use to speak to a work colleague. And you shouldn't even speak to each work colleague the exact same way.

Remember that much of communication is nonverbal. People often get more meaning from your expression than they do your words. Your appearance and everything else they see and hear says something to them. Create the environment that reflects how you want your team, family, or friends to feel and act. Be as purposeful about what the environment communicates as you are the words you choose.

It's Not Just How, but When and Where You Communicate

If you are married, my guess is that you have experienced a day like this:

You're up early to prepare for a last-minute meeting that was called for 8:00 a.m. regarding a new problem with an important customer. After the meeting, you spend the rest of the day behind a closed door with two coworkers creating a presentation to show the customer how you're going to resolve the issue. You work so hard that you don't realize until 2:30 that you haven't eaten lunch, and by that time the cafe is closed, so you eat a lunch consisting of food from the vending machine.

After work, you speed to the park to pick up your daughter from soccer practice and then order the most nutritious sounding items at the drive through. Once home, you put the foil-wrapped food on plates to pass as some semblance of a family meal. After dinner, your son remembers that he has a project due at school tomorrow that he hasn't started, so after running to the store to buy poster board, glue, and glitter, you spend an hour reading to him off of Wikipedia about the Industrial Revolution while he draws. You make sure the kids are bathed and in bed. You brush your teeth, get in bed, and pull a book off your nightstand, but quickly realize you're too tired to read. Then, just as you reach over to turn out the bedside light, you hear this from your spouse who is lying next to you: "So, something you said the other day really bothered me, and I'd like to talk about it."

Seriously? Now?

There is a time and a place for everything. The environment matters.

34
Seek to Understand

In Chapter 12, "Others Before Self," I referenced this habit from Stephen Covey's *7 Habits of Highly Effective People*. I believe it is so important that it merits further discussion here.

Covey's actual statement is: "Seek first to understand, then to be understood." But in my opinion, the power of this concept lies in the first phrase. Seeking first to understand is powerful in many aspects of life—not just in relationships.

In general, salespeople have bad reputations. The profession as a whole has a bit of a negative stigma about it. So bad, that we come up with all kinds of creative names to avoid calling them salespeople: business development, account manager, customer consultant, you name it. Why do you think this is?

John Steinbeck has a fantastic chapter in *The Grapes of Wrath* that is told from the perspective of a used car dealer who sells jalopies to dislocated farmers crossing the country in search of work. Reading this will make you never want to buy another used car, but further, it confirms every suspicion you've ever had about the people who sell these cars. They are trying to get you to spend your money on something by misrepresenting what they have as something that you need.

The stereotype of a salesperson is someone who has something to sell, and through trickery and pressure, will convince you that you need or want it. Whether you actually need or want it is irrelevant. Later, after you've bought it and realize that you parted with your money for some useless junk, you are angry but have no recourse.

No wonder we hate salespeople.

The problem of course is that this is a short-term game. This kind of salesperson never gets a repeat customer and eventually runs out of suckers.

I would argue that by seeking first to understand, a salesperson can actually have a much easier career in sales (and one with more friends). If I truly understand what you need or want, I can present my product or service to you in a way that solves that need. If it doesn't solve your need, then you won't buy and I won't sell. But if I can really solve your problem, then chances are, you will be my customer time and again, and you'll likely tell others about my product. And as any salesperson will tell you, referrals are the easiest and quickest sales.

In some cases, you may be able to pressure me into buying something I don't want, but for the most part, you better be able to provide something I really need if you hope to get my business.

But salespeople are not the only ones who make this mistake. All of us, at some point, have to convince someone to do something that we need—to act a certain way, to stop doing a certain thing, or to simply listen to us. And most of the time, we use some of the same tactics as the cheesy sales guy—we try to overwhelm them with information about it, tell them how good for them this will ultimately be, refer to all the other people who are also doing it, or guilt them into it because of how much we need it. (These are all techniques taught to salespeople!)

These conversations go very differently when you really understand the other person, and the same is true in sales. When you know what is important to the customer, what their goals are, and what they believe, you can frame your offer in a much more effective way.

Let's step away from sales for a minute. In Chapter 12, I referenced an argument I once had where we weren't even arguing about the same thing, but it took us an hour to figure that out because we weren't listening to each other. We were too busy articulating our own arguments to hear what the other was saying. I would submit that most arguments fall into this category. We don't understand the context and assumptions of the other person; we only hear their conclusions. So we argue over conclusions that will never reconcile because we have different sets of facts.

The mental process of moving from facts to conclusions (and then actions) is described by author Chris Argyris as "The Ladder of Inference." We go from being presented with a set of facts, to filtering those facts through our experiences, then applying assumptions to those facts, forming beliefs about them, and then making decisions based on the reality we've created around those facts.

Researcher and author Brené Brown coined a wonderful phrase that, I think, summarizes this process. She calls it "the story I am telling myself right now." We take that limited data set of "facts," and our brain puts together a story so that we can make sense of our environment. The problem is that we rarely have all of the facts, so we fill in the blanks with assumptions and draw conclusions based on our limited information and senses. We end up with a story that gets us excited, angry, depressed, or any other emotion you can name. Here is an example:

One time a manager asked to meet with me. Once we started, she proceeded to ask me if she could move to a job in another one of our companies. I asked her which job she had in mind.

"Well, I don't know yet. I wanted to see if there was anything you knew about that you think I'd be a good candidate for."

"Why do you want to leave your current role?"

"I just don't think that I fit in there. I don't think it is the place for me."

I'll spare you the next 20 minutes of dialog where I asked question after question trying to get her to open up to me about the real issue. I finally got her to admit that she had messed up a project and that several people knew about it. Subsequently, there were some management meetings she hadn't been invited to. Finally, she had recently learned her manager was recommending someone else for a promotion.

"I just know that with this hanging over my head there is no way that I am going to get another promotion," she explained. "I have no career path left in my current company."

"So, let's talk about the story that you are telling yourself."

"What?"

"Here is what you know: you screwed up a project that was pretty visible in the company, there were meetings you weren't invited to (which it turns out, other people weren't invited to either), and someone else got a promotion (that you weren't eligible for anyway). So, you have put these pieces of information together to conclude that the view of you among leadership is that you have topped out and will never be able to take on more responsibility. They are now cutting you out of meetings and promoting other people above you. That is the story you are telling yourself."

"Well, yeah, I guess so."

"Let me ask you. Why did you come to me about this? Why didn't you go to your boss or the person who runs your company?"

"Well, I didn't think he would recommend me for another job since he thinks I don't have potential."

"Has he ever told you that?"

"Well, no, but it's obvious based on his actions."

"What I should do is end this conversation now and direct you to go ask him. But I know that you won't do that, so I'm going to tell you what is really going on. Yes, you did fail at that project. However, we love it around here when people fail. The more spectacularly the better because it gives us a chance to see how you will respond. Failing is easy. Getting back off the ground, learning from your failure, and bravely getting back to work is what is hard. What's more, as a leader, it is important that you have failed so you know how to support the people you lead when they fail. The truth of the matter is that I just had a conversation with Bob last week. He actually thinks you have a lot of potential, which is why he gave you that difficult project. He is anxiously awaiting to see what you learn from this and how you handle the failure.

"The meeting you weren't invited to and the promotion were just random events that have absolutely nothing to do with you. But because you have constructed this story in your head, you are looking for data that confirms your theory."

She sat in stunned silence.

"Now, go talk to your manager and talk to Bob. And next time you think you have figured out what is going on, I would encourage you to go right to the source to confirm it before you get so worked up that you are ready to look for another job."

Please let me say at this point that there have been plenty of times when I screwed up this "Seek to Understand" concept, but this time—I nailed it. Let's look at this situation.

First, if I hadn't taken the time to really delve into what was going on and just acted on her initial request to help her find a new job, it would have been bad all around. The company she currently worked for would have missed her, and she would not have learned anything from the situation.

Second, this whole thing started because she hadn't sought to understand what other people really thought. She came up with an erroneous story based on limited information and then acted on it.

Third, her boss also had some culpability here. I asked her if he had spoken to her about the failed project since it happened. "Not really and not directly about the project," she said. It doesn't take much empathy to figure out that someone who had just experienced that kind of public failure would start fearing for their job and get to where this young lady had gone to emotionally. If he had sought to understand how she was feeling, he could have had the same conversation I had with her and averted the whole mess.

Part of seeking to understand is knowing that often people don't understand themselves. They don't always know what they want, much less what they need. Occasionally, because of additional knowledge, or because you aren't emotionally involved, you may be able gain insight that leads to understanding them better than they understand themselves. Customers don't always understand what they want and neither do people at work or in our families. Seeking to understand means that you go on the journey of understanding with them.

Communicate Problems Directly

The other problem in the story here is that this associate didn't go directly to the people involved to discuss her issue. This is very common. A coworker says something that I think is rude. I want to talk about it, so I go to another teammate, my boyfriend, my mom, my sister, and then yet another teammate. Perhaps all of these people serve a purpose in letting me vent, and maybe they even give me some good advice, but you know what they cannot do? None of them can solve the problem.

Unless you have a legitimate fear of reprisal or physical harm, it is always better to talk directly to the other people involved in the problem. Obviously, you need to approach the conversation seeking to understand versus attacking and accusing. If it still doesn't go well, and it's a real problem, then get someone else involved who can actually help (like your boss). But the first step should always be addressing the issue with the people involved. More than likely, it will be the only step needed.

35
Declare Facts and Opinions

The quality of your decisions is a direct result of the quality of the information you have to make those decisions. If you have perfect information all the time, you will make pretty good decisions. When you have no clue what is going on, it's hard to know what you should do.

Anyone who has ever managed a salesperson has heard this statement: "We have to lower our price. All our customers are going to our competitor because they have a lower price."

Now first of all, anytime I hear "all" or "everyone," alarms start going off everywhere. That means there is an overgeneralization on the loose.

"Okay, well how many customers have told you they are leaving us for our competitor?"

"Well, just a few, but I'm sure they are all thinking about it."

"How many is a few?"

"Well...two."

"Okay. And both of those customers said they were leaving because the competitor's price was lower? They used those words?"

"Well, no, not those words exactly."

"What did they say?"

"One said that he was considering another vendor because their pricing looked better."

"What did the other one say?"

"They said that they couldn't meet with me next week because they have a meeting with another vendor."

"They didn't say anything about pricing?"

"No, not specifically, but why else would they meet with another vendor?"

"Perhaps it's worth asking them to find out."

I could use this story as another example of the importance of seeking to understand. The salesperson needs to seek to understand what is really going on with his client. And thank goodness the sales manager took the time to dig deeper and didn't react to the initial claim that all their customers were leaving. But, let's pretend that the salesperson did seek to understand, and then there was a conversation that went something like this:

Sales guy to his manager: "I think that we have an issue where our competitor is undercutting our prices, and some of our customers are considering moving to them."

Sales manager: "What makes you think that?"

"Well, I can't prove it, but a few things have happened that point to it. First, one customer flat out told me that they were considering another vendor whose pricing looked better. I asked him what he meant by that, and he wouldn't elaborate much, just saying it was different enough that he needed to look into it. I asked a second customer about meeting next week, and he said he couldn't because he had a meeting with that same vendor. This is a pretty price conscious customer, so I am guessing that a lower price would get them to move. Again, I don't know anything for sure yet, but this is my opinion based on the information I have."

Exact same conversations, but totally different level of usefulness for the manager. First, let's pretend that in the first scenario, the manager took the initial statement at face value that "all of their customers were going to a competitor because they had a lower price." The salesperson declared it as a fact, and so the manager takes it as fact. Well, if you know that your customers are in fact leaving you because of your high price, what should you do? More than likely, you will lower your prices. Call our customers and tell them that we will discount our price by 10% if they stay with us!

In the second scenario, the salesperson relayed the same basic information about the conversations with the customers, but the conclusion that customers would leave them for a lower priced competitor was presented as an opinion. This is very different, and as a manager, you now have a different set of options to pursue. Perhaps you seek ways to better understand what those customers really need. You would try to figure out exactly what this new lower pricing was (if in fact it existed). You might start calling other customers to see if anyone else was talking to the vendor, etc.

Now, this is not to say that opinions should never be considered in decision making. In reality, when making tough decisions we often have very few facts at our disposal, and so opinions become important—especially if they are the opinions of people we trust. The point is that as a decision maker, you want to know the difference. Facts impact decisions differently than opinions, and when people disguise their opinions as facts, it negatively impacts the decision that is made.

Here is another example:

"The client will only agree to their contract language—not ours."

I know there isn't much context here, but if you are presented with this statement of fact, what choices do you have? Well, it's pretty binary—either take their language or don't sign the contract.

But consider that same statement made this way:

"The client has rejected our changes to the contract and said they want to go back to their original language. I haven't spoken to them yet, but my opinion is that we are nearing the end of our ability to negotiate."

Well, that's different. We may yet get down to that binary choice of sign their language or not, but we do still have some other options open to us.

This disguising of opinions as facts plays out in relationships also. Any parent ever heard this kind of statement?

"The coach doesn't want me on the team."

What do you do if you are presented with the fact that the coach of your child's sports team does not want her on the team? Well, you either tell her to gut it out until the coach kicks her off, or go ahead and quit now. Of course, this smells like a story that your daughter is telling herself, so you ask, "Did the coach tell you she doesn't want you on the team?"

"No, but she didn't put me in at the end of the game, so she obviously doesn't think I'm good enough to play and doesn't want me on the team."

As a parent, the fact that your child believes (has an opinion) that her coach doesn't want her on the team is a problem that you have to deal with. But it is a very different problem than if her coach actually told her that she doesn't want her on the team.

Get in the habit of recognizing when you know something as fact versus your conclusion based on the evidence you have seen. Then in conversations—especially those in which a decision has to be made—make a distinction between the things you know as facts versus your opinions regarding those facts. Facts and opinions are both important, but they impact our decisions differently.

Be Honest with Yourself

It's understandable that you don't want everyone to know the absolute truth about you all the time. We all have an image we try to uphold—the picture we want people to have of us versus the ugly truths we know about ourselves. Hopefully you have at least one person in your life who knows your dark side and loves you regardless. Someone with whom you can be really honest. But even more important than being honest with someone else is being honest with yourself.

Take the time to analyze and get in touch with what is really going on in your life. Ask yourself what story you are telling yourself, and then look at the assumptions that are driving that story to determine if they are actual facts or conclusions you have drawn. Are your choices being driven by your professed values or a different set of values? What are you really feeling right now, and why do you feel that way?

You can't make a good decision if you don't have the right facts. And you aren't going to achieve your goals if you aren't honest with yourself about why you do what you do.

There is peace that comes when there is harmony between the public you and private you. If you aren't yet ready to be honest with the rest of the world about who you are, at least be honest with yourself.

36
Principles are Sacrosanct; Methods are Not

As you contemplate all the maxims and lessons contained in this book, I encourage you to consider them through the lens that principles are sacrosanct, but methods are not. The core values and beliefs I have tried to articulate are ones that are really important to us and largely inviolable. However, the way we apply them is not the same by team, by leader, or even at different points in time.

Markets are changing at an unprecedented pace. New and different kinds of competitors appear constantly in every industry. The way customers expect to engage with our company is continually evolving. The solutions and practices of yesterday are often the wrong ones for tomorrow.

We have to be careful that we focus on the principles behind the practices we have today and not the practices themselves. If we focus only on how we do things and forget why we're doing them that way, we lock ourselves into systems that will soon become outdated. Business models, organizational structures, compensation plans—everything must be constantly held up for scrutiny. Those systems were all created in the past, and the assumptions that led to the creation of those systems are instantly outdated. But the principles behind why and how the systems or practices were created almost never change.

I could take any one of the beliefs outlined in this book and point to a business practice we have that is a direct result. I could also show you how that belief was applied differently in different periods of our company's growth.

There are a tremendous number of judgments that leaders and managers must make. We are put into situations daily where we must plot a course and there is no obvious or easy answer. Discernment is an incredibly valuable quality for a leader.

Perhaps the most difficult decisions a leader must make involve change. What should be consistent and what can have variation? What things in our businesses are so core that they should always be the same, and what are the things that should evolve as the world changes?

In our business, almost none of our business practices or systems are unalterable. We want to constantly challenge what we do and reevaluate if there is a better way. This is an incredibly tough concept for most people to believe.

As a leader, one of the hardest judgments to make is when to let someone you are leading make a choice you wouldn't make. It's not a wrong choice and you couldn't really label it as a mistake, it's just a different way of doing things.

In Chapter 10, I gave an example of a manager who uses quarterly objectives to manage his team. He gets increased responsibility and is charged with supervising a manager who prefers semiannual goals with the team he manages. The first manager has a decision as to whether he should force the second one to switch to quarterly instead of semiannual goals.

Certainly, there are many factors that go into this equation (such as if there are standards used throughout the company), but the question remains: is the belief in quarterly goals important enough to insist upon change?

This may seem like a rather trivial issue, but these types of decisions come up routinely and, in sum, can become big deals. Should I force my team to use the same kind of time management system? Should I insist they enter information into the database the same way? Do I give my salespeople leeway on using different sales presentations, or should they all use the same one? Where do you allow for personal style and where don't you?

In both of these types of scenarios, I have tried to apply the maxim that principles are sacrosanct, methods are not. In other words, there are some principles that we won't break, but the way we apply those principles can vary.

You have to allow for style in the way that leaders run their teams and relate to their people. So when I am faced with a leader who wants to do something differently from the way I would do it or different from existing company practice, I first consider whether the action will accomplish what we want to accomplish in a way that is consistent with our values and beliefs. If it will, and I don't think allowing the inconsistency of practice with other teams will cause a problem, then I'll allow it.

It is so easy to get locked into the business models and practices of today. Maintaining the status quo is the easiest path, while forcing or embracing change creates friction that requires more energy to overcome. But business models change—sometimes quickly. We must be wise in judging what should change and what should not.

37
Be Well

One time a friend challenged me to write my own eulogy. After determining that this wasn't part of a plot he had to kill me, I became intrigued and got the rest of the instructions. Imagine you die 30 or 40 years from now (time doesn't matter, the point is that it is in the distant future). First, who would you like to deliver your eulogy? Now write out the speech that you would like them to give at your funeral.

So, if you are game, I suggest that right now you put this book down and accept this challenge. Grab a pen or keyboard and write out the eulogy you want to be said about you at your future funeral. Don't read ahead before you write the eulogy. Only read the rest after you are done writing. Got it? Then stop reading…now.

Really, don't read any further.

Are you done?

Okay, you can start reading again.

What emotions did you feel? For me, it was emotional just to think about who would give my eulogy, much less what they would say.

Now, I want you to do one more thing. You don't have to write this one down, but I do want you to put the book down and think about these questions:

What would your eulogy be if you died today?

How different is that from the one you hope to have said about you in the future?

You don't have to tell anyone else about this (although it would be great if you can), but now is the ideal time to practice being honest with yourself. And frankly, if you aren't going to be honest with yourself in this exercise, it will be a waste of time. So, go for it.

My guess is that there are at least some things that you would want said about you in the future that are different from what would be said today.

Your eulogy represents the legacy of your life. It summarizes who you were and what you left behind. This exercise forces you to not only define success for your life but also think about the way you want to live while you pursue that success.

The good news is that more than likely, you have some time left to reconcile these two eulogies. You can start living in a way that is more consistent with the values you want to hold dear. You can start doing things that move you toward achieving your personal mission—your definition of success for your life. You can start being aware of your decisions as to how you spend your time, how you prioritize your activities, and how you relate to other people. That's the good news.

The bad news is that there is no guarantee as to how much time you do have left. You may have imagined your funeral 30 years from now, but it may actually be only days away. That doesn't mean there is no hope; it simply means there is no time to waste.

A few years ago, our company launched a new name to encompass all of our wellness programs. While we were coming up with this brand, we sent out a one question survey to our associates asking, "What does it mean to you to be well?"

We received amazing answers. The words were so beautiful, we took them and covered an entire wall in the restaurant at our corporate headquarters.

But what struck me about the answers was the variation. People tend to think about wellness from the point of view of health—talking about diet and exercise. Those things are important but only a small part of being well. And our associates got that. They used words like relationships, gratitude, achievement, challenge, and energy.

My guess is that as you consider your legacy and as you define success for your life, you do not have a one-dimensional definition either.

Wellness is a hard word to define, but I think the National Wellness Institute does a good job of capturing its elements:

> "Wellness is a conscious, self-directed and evolving process
> of achieving full potential. Wellness is multidimensional and
> holistic, encompassing lifestyle, mental and spiritual well-
> being and the environment. Wellness is positive and affirming."

We only get one chance to experience life on this earth. There will never be another today, and there will never be another you to experience today. You cannot change who you are today—your actions of the past determined that. But you can choose actions today that can change who you are tomorrow. The question is, who will you choose to be?

Leaders have a choice as to how they lead. My definition of success, the legacy I want to leave in my life, is that I utilize my influence as a leader to help people achieve wellness in their lives. This mission reflects my values and my beliefs about the responsibility of stewardship that has been entrusted to me.

But regardless of whether we are in a position of leadership, everyone has this power of influence in someone's life. That influence can be used to help improve the lives of others—or not.

My hope and prayer is that you also choose a life of wellness and that part of your legacy will be the service of bringing about wellness in others.

The purpose of this book is to help our leaders—those most responsible for ensuring the future success of our companies—understand the things that *don't* change: the values and beliefs which shaped the actions that have created the culture of today. Only by understanding these values and beliefs can our leaders know what actions to take tomorrow. Those actions are what will sustain our culture.

I pray that all our future leaders develop wisdom in discerning the principles that are sacrosanct and the methods that are temporary applications of those principles.

The values and beliefs that my father instilled in our company from the beginning are the same ones that will sustain us far into the future. May we all develop extraordinary abilities to apply them appropriately and consistently.

Referenced Works

"About Wellness." National Wellness Institute. http://www.
nationalwellness.org/AboutWellness

Argyris, Chris. *Overcoming Organizational Defenses: Facilitating Organizational Learning*. Pearson, 1990.

Blanchard, Ken, Patricia Zigarmi, and Drea Zigarmi. *Leadership and the One Minute Manager: Increasing Effectiveness Through Situational Leadership*. New York: William Morrow, 1985.

Brown, Brené. *Rising Strong*. New York: Spiegel & Grau, 2015.

Connors, Roger, and Tom Smith. *Change the Culture, Change the Game: The Breakthrough Strategy for Energizing Your Organization and Creating Accountability for Results*. New York: The Penguin Group, 2011.

Covey, Stephen R. *7 Habits of Highly Effective People: Powerful Lessons in Personal Change, Revised edition*. New York: Free Press, 2004.

Green, Joey. *The Road to Success is Paved with Failure: How Hundreds of Famous People Triumphed Over Inauspicious Beginnings, Crushing rejection, Humiliating Defeats and Other Speed Bumps Along Life's Highway*. Little, Brown, 2001.

Hersey, Dr. Paul. *The Situational Leader, Fourth Edition*. Warner Books, 1985.

Lencioni, Patrick. *Death By Meeting: A Leadership Fable About Solving the Most Painful Problem in Business*. San Francisco: Jossey-Bass, 2004.

McChesney, Chris, Sean Covey, and Jim Huling. *The 4 Disciplines of Execution: Achieving Your Wildly Important Goals*. London: Simon & Schuster UK, 2012.

Schaffer, Robert H. and Ronald N. Ashkenas. *Rapid Results! How 100-Day Projects Build the Capacity for Large-Scale Change*. San Francisco: Jossey-Bass, 2005.

Schein, Edgar H. *Organizational Culture and Leadership*. San Francisco: Jossey-Bass, 2010.

Steinbeck, John. *The Grapes of Wrath, Reissue edition*. New York: Penguin Classics, 2006.

Tice, Lou. *Smart Talk For Achieving Your Potential: 5 Steps to Get You From Here to There*. Seattle: Pacific Institute Publishing, 2005.

Made in the USA
Columbia, SC
17 April 2018